BUSINESS START-UPS MADE E-Z

MADE E-Z PRODUCTS, Inc.
Deerfield Beach, Florida / www.MadeE-Z.com

NOTICE:

THIS PRODUCT IS NOT INTENDED TO PROVIDE LEGAL ADVICE. IT CONTAINS GENERAL INFORMATION FOR EDUCATIONAL PURPOSES ONLY. PLEASE CONSULT AN ATTORNEY IN ALL LEGAL MATTERS. THIS PRODUCT WAS NOT NECESSARILY PREPARED BY A PERSON LICENSED TO PRACTICE LAW IN THIS STATE.

Important Notice

Table of contents

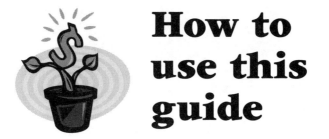

How to use this guide

E-Z Legal's Made E-Z™ Guides can help you achieve an important legal objective conveniently, efficiently and economically. But it is important to properly use this guide if you are to avoid later difficulties.

◆ Carefully read all information, warnings and disclaimers concerning the legal forms in this guide. If after thorough examination you decide that you have circumstances that are not covered by the forms in this guide, or you do not feel confident about preparing your own documents, consult an attorney.

◆ Complete each blank on each legal form. Do not skip over inapplicable blanks or lines intended to be completed. If the blank is inapplicable, mark "N/A" or "None" or use a dash. This shows you have not overlooked the item.

◆ Always use pen or type on legal documents—never use pencil.

◆ Avoid erasures and "cross-outs" on final documents. Use photocopies of each document as worksheets, or as final copies. All documents submitted to the court must be printed on one side only.

◆ Correspondence forms may be reproduced on your own letterhead if you prefer.

◆ Whenever legal documents are to be executed by a partnership or corporation, the signatory should designate his or her title.

◆ It is important to remember that on legal contracts or agreements between parties all terms and conditions must be clearly stated. Provisions may not be enforceable unless in writing. All parties to the agreement should receive a copy.

◆ Instructions contained in this guide are for your benefit and protection, so follow them closely.

◆ You will find a glossary of useful terms at the end of this guide. Refer to this glossary if you encounter unfamiliar terms.

◆ Always keep legal documents in a safe place and in a location known to your spouse, family, personal representative or attorney.

Introduction to Business Start-ups Made E-Z™

Small business growth is booming. A million new businesses will be born this year alone. For most Americans, the lure is obvious: the glimmering prospect of self-made fortune. As a wage earner, it seems you are rarely paid what you are worth. You may devote your efforts to generating profits for your boss only to receive the simple security of "regular" employment. When you become a business owner, you ascend to the top of the fiscal food chain. However, your rewards will be only as great as your company's success.

Like preparing a good meal, everything runs smoothly if you are prepared ahead of time: The great chefs have their vegetables sliced and meat marinated before they even turned on the stove, to make sure the meal comes out as good as it possibly could. It's no different than starting your own business; if you do your preparation work well, your business will run better and be more profitable. That's what this guide's all about—we give you the tools and information you need to take that million-dollar idea and make your business a reality.

Starting your own business will take a lot of hard work, a handful of imagination, some creative financing, and a little bit of luck—everything else you need is in this guide, made E-Z!

Starting a new business

Chapter 1

Starting a new business

You're ready to take on the challenge of starting your own business and being your own boss. Great! But it should be clear from the beginning that it will not be as easy as it sounds, and that the money will not roll in overnight. You are about to make a commitment of time, energy and money of such immense proportions that you may even lose sight of the dream that has inspired you to purchase this guide in the first place. But if you heed the advice in these pages and work hard, you *will* have a business you can be proud of!

There is no denying that starting a new business (or even maintaining an established one) is as difficult as it is rewarding. Keep this in mind: You will probably exhaust all your time and finances just to get your business rolling, then wait . . . and wait for your investment to pay off. Most companies don't break even until the first six months—at the very earliest. And before you feast on any of the profits, you must pay all the bills, from rent to inventory, from

> **note** How small a salary can you survive on until profits appear? Weigh all potential gains against potential risks on both a personal and professional level when deciding to start a new business.

materials to insurance and utilities. Along with all rags-to-riches success stories are overwhelming failure rates: *80 percent of new companies will not last five years; a third will not survive even the first year.* Being your own boss is a risk you must be well-prepared to take.

Beyond the hope of riches are several intrinsic attractions: control over your own destiny, pursuing an interest you truly enjoy and realizing a dream. It may be your chance to finally escape that oppressive boss, robotic schedule and lack of meaningful responsibilities that comes with working for someone else. In your own company, you face all the exciting challenges and make all the important decisions. At the same time, you must also shoulder many of the mundane tasks—from keeping the books to sweeping floors—as your company gets its feet on the ground. Forget all about the concept of a 9-to-5, 40-hour workweek. Your business may not only demand odd hours. It may also consume every waking minute and cause countless sleepless nights.

You may possess an encyclopedic knowledge of your industry—from accounting methods to marketing to production—and still not be able to effectively manage a business. Can you

> **E-Z TIP** In running your own business, you will persevere only if you enjoy what you do.

make tough decisions? Do you have leadership skills? Are you a people person? Imagine yourself motivating a staff of employees and making sure customers are satisfied. If the feeling makes you uncomfortable, perhaps you should reconsider. A large percentage of failures are due to incompetent, ill-informed or unprepared management.

Finding the right fit

Blind ambition lures hoards of people into businesses they know nothing about. Following their dreams, enterprising housewives start interior decorating firms and store clerks open restaurants. Some do well, but the majority fail. You should be drawn not by your dream but by your clear vision, distinct knowledge and broad experience. Pursue something you can enjoy, manage and profit from. Whether you wish to start a business in the service, sales or manufacturing sector, investigate all aspects of the business before committing your time and finances to it. If it is not already your career, try freelancing, attending night classes or seminars, or learn the tricks of the trade from those in the know. Two-thirds of all new businesses begin as a part-time pursuit.

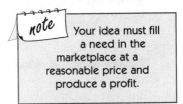 Your idea must fill a need in the marketplace at a reasonable price and produce a profit.

Do you have a winning idea? A new business concept may fill you with frenzied enthusiasm, but will the concept seem as exciting when presented to potential investors and the buying public? Make sure your confidence is justified.

Four deadly myths

Success never comes easy. Yet if you have a good idea and are hard working, ambitious and patient, you can probably make it on your own. Beware believing these four common "success killers" that keep the masses toiling for others:

1) *You need to be born a shifty-eyed, smooth-talking entrepreneur.* Preparation, leadership and common sense are more practical skills for survival.

2) *You need a fortune to make a fortune.* To prosper, you need to be resourceful and willing to take risks.

3) *You need to fear debt.* By financing your start-up costs with as little of your money down as possible, you can protect your personal assets while keeping them in reserve to help out in a time of need. Without leverage, you may never have enough inventory or working capital to make a profit.

4) *You need to hire a full staff of accountants, lawyers and personnel managers.* While some procedures require a professional, you can learn to handle most routine tasks yourself if you are organized and flexible.

Two rules to remember

Most businesses fail because they fell short of unrealistic expectations.

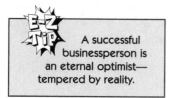

A successful businessperson is an eternal optimist— tempered by reality.

Planning for the worst will prepare you the best. Richard Sheldon, a Harvard MBA and prosperous Connecticut businessman, offers two simple but insightful adages known as Sheldon's Laws:

1) **Things take three times as long as predicted.** Bureaucracy, paperwork and other priorities inevitably delay even the most conservative deadlines.

2) **Things cost twice as much as predicted.** Maintenance fees, telephone bills, office supplies, marketing expenses, bad debt and collection costs typically add up well beyond meticulously calculated budgets.

Can your plan work? Answers will emerge only after developing a thorough business plan that details everything from market research to budget, pricing, location and staffing, and overall projections. Keep the above rules in mind as you proceed.

What you'll find in this guide

This product guides you through all aspects of starting your own business. First, we will take you step-by-step through the basics of a Business Plan, the all-important document you will use to construct and guide your business. Part one of your Business Plan will address the basic goals and direction for your business. Part two will focus more closely on the following components:

- a solid Legal Structure to protect your assets and allow you maximum tax benefits

- a Marketing Plan that connects you with customers and clients

- a Financial Plan to determine how much money you need . . . and where you'll find it

- an Operational Plan that tackles vital setup issues such as finding an effective location, bargaining for equipment, obtaining business insurance and others

Begin company operations with basic but essential accounting, tax and personnel pointers. You also have access to helpful, free or low-cost resources, plus a vital collection of sample forms, worksheets and agreements. Starting your own business is an awesome challenge, but one you can conquer with a little help. Good fortunes!

The Business Plan

Chapter 2
The Business Plan

What you'll find in this chapter:

➠ How a Business Plan will help you

➠ The elements of a Business Plan

➠ Statement of Purpose

➠ Your business description

➠ The other Plans that you will need

Why you need a Business Plan

A well-researched Business Plan is the chief tool for organizing your ideas and communicating them to others. It encompasses your complete sales pitch for your new enterprise. You should also write a business plan any time you contemplate change: restructuring, relocating or expanding. A thorough business plan is absolutely essential for three reasons:

1) *It allows you to objectively analyze your chances of success.* Too many entrepreneurs rush in without proper planning, only to discover they are fighting a losing battle. The

E-Z TIP
Scrutinize your proposal for strengths and weaknesses, continually implementing improvements as you go.

more you know, the better prepared you are for the future. Thoroughly analyze your idea in terms of potential customers, competition, marketing and operating strategies and your bottom line.

2) *It offers solid objectives and strategies.* An effective business plan is by no means a static document. It is a dynamic pattern for success that continually evolves as your business grows, structuring decisions based upon objective standards.

3) *It helps you secure financing.* You must sell your business to potential lenders, suppliers, and distributors, who will treat your proposal as an investment—they will look for proof of profits. Most are trained in spotting weak points in a business plan, and can easily detect them if your research is not rigorous and thorough.

note A solid Business Plan promotes the knowledge and confidence needed to close a sale, whether you are starting a business, launching new products or entering new markets.

A complete Business Plan explores all aspects of your start-up and continuing operation. It answers every question—who, what, where, when, why, how, and how much—you or prospective investors can possibly anticipate. Some experts suggest spending between 250 and 500 hours researching, developing and revising your plan. Equally important is organizing and condensing it into a clear, concise and compelling presentation. Superfluous data will bog down your plan.

The whole process may seem a bit overwhelming at first, but be patient. A well-developed plan can mean the difference between penthouse and poorhouse as your dream takes shape.

The Business Plan, Part One

Cover Page

Begin your Business Plan with a professional-looking cover page. This should feature the company name, address and phone number. A sharp logo, product picture and/or compelling slogan can help capture the image you wish to convey. An amateurish cover can forestall an otherwise strong campaign.

Table of Contents

This saves time by directing prospective investors and others to the information they need.

Statement of Purpose

This brief overview should be no more than a page or two. State your company's purpose and objectives, addressing the market demand and unique strategies you will use to successfully satisfy that demand. Indicate the type of business entity you will choose or have chosen. List all principals' names, addresses and areas of expertise. Explain what capital and assets you will contribute, and the cost of the items you need to finance. Provide a short description of the products and services you will offer as well as a concise overview of your competition. Keep it simple and compelling; attack the details later.

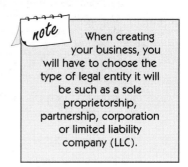

note

When creating your business, you will have to choose the type of legal entity it will be such as a sole proprietorship, partnership, corporation or limited liability company (LLC).

Business Description

You presented a rough sketch of your company in the Statement of Purpose section. Now fill in the details. Explain who you are and why you are starting a business. Present concrete advantages that will convince the reader you will succeed—based on experience, innovation or opportunity.

♦ Describe what type of business you will be engaged in: sales, manufacturing or service. Briefly describe the type of products or services you will offer, when and where you plan to open, and the number of employees you initially will hire.

♦ Specify which type of business entity you will form. Will you be a sole proprietorship, partnership, corporation or LLC? What advantages does this chosen business entity offer? When will you register, and in what state?

♦ Detail your line of products and/or services. Are they new, unique or otherwise different from anything else currently on the market? Describe what you are offering in terms of the target market and the price, selection, service, quantity and quality of your goods and services.

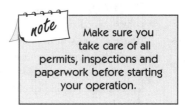

note Make sure you take care of all permits, inspections and paperwork before starting your operation.

♦ Explain the facilities and equipment you will need. Where are you planning to locate? Will you rent, lease or buy, and why? What specific advantages does the site offer in terms of traffic, clientele, safety, accessibility and efficiency? What equipment do you need, how much will it cost and how long will it last?

♦ Discuss your daily operations. What will be your hours of operation? Do you plan to reach customers through retailer, wholesale outlets or through direct mail? Will you pick up, deliver or make house calls? Will you have an answering service, a beeper or a cellular phone? What type of system will you use for inventory and quality control? What type of customer service policies will you institute?

♦ What type of management structure will you deploy? How will you find your employees? Do you plan to contract work out to freelancers and independent contractors? Outline positions, pay, benefits and policies.

♦ What kinds of professional help will you require? Will you hire a lawyer, an accountant, or both? What type of insurance will you use? What government and industry regulations apply to your business and how will you comply with them?

The Business Plan, Part Two

Your Marketing Plan

• Discuss the products/services offered.

• Identify the customer demand for your product/service.

• Identify your market, its size and locations.

• Explain how your product/service will be advertised and marketed.

• Explain the pricing strategy.

For a complete overview, please see chapter 4, "The Marketing Plan."

Your Financial Plan

- Explain the source and amount of the business' initial capital.

- Develop a monthly operating budget for the first year.

- Project the expected return on investment, or ROI, and monthly cash flow for the first year.

- Provide projected income statements and balance sheets for a two-year period.

- Discuss your break-even point.

- Explain your personal balance sheet

- Detail your method of compensation.

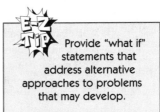

Provide "what if" statements that address alternative approaches to problems that may develop.

- Discuss who will maintain your accounting records and how they will be kept.

For a complete overview, please see chapter 5, "The Financial Plan."

Your Operational Plan

- Explain how the business will be managed on a day-to-day basis.

- Discuss hiring and personnel procedures.

- Discuss insurance, lease or rent agreements, and related issues pertinent to your business.

- Describe the equipment necessary to produce your products or services.

- Account for production and delivery of products and services.

For a complete overview, please see chapter 8, "The Operational Plan."

Your Conclusion

Summarize your business goals and objectives and express your commitment to the success of your business.

The structure of your business

3

Chapter 3

The structure of
your business

What you'll find in this chapter:

➠ Why choosing the right entity is important

➠ The corporation

➠ The S corporation

➠ The limited liability company (LLC)

➠ Choosing a name for your company

Will your business be a sole proprietorship, partnership, S or C corporation, or limited liability company? Short-term considerations include structural regulations, filing fees and record-keeping requirements. These are the things that will affect you daily as you run your business.

More importantly, consider long-term factors such as tax benefits, raising capital, transferal of interests and asset protection. Owners of over three million unincorporated American businesses risk having their personal assets plundered by lawsuits, creditors, bankruptcy, the IRS, even probate and divorce. Many of these bold adventurers end up with nothing and thus never rebound to try again.

note Over half of all entrepreneurs start their ventures as either sole proprietorships or partnerships, leaving their personal assets fully exposed to business creditors.

Although you may believe you will never fail, the fact is your company has only a 20 percent chance of surviving beyond five years. Others mistakenly feel incorporating is reserved for giant companies employing hundreds and grossing millions. But even single-person companies are eligible for, and should consider, corporate protection. You can easily obtain the proper forms from your state's Department of Incorporation or from any office supply store carrying E-Z Legal products, and fill them out and file them with the Secretary of State on your own.

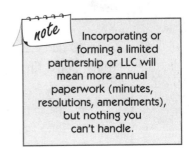

note Incorporating or forming a limited partnership or LLC will mean more annual paperwork (minutes, resolutions, amendments), but nothing you can't handle.

Given the proper forms and simple instructions, you can easily form your own corporation, S corporation, limited liability company or limited partnership, each offering distinct benefits. Consider the advantages and disadvantages of each described below.

The corporation

DEFINITION

A *corporation* is formed and authorized by law to act as a single entity, although it may be owned by one or more persons. It is legally endowed with rights and responsibilities and has a life of its own independent of the owners and operators. It has been defined by the United States Supreme Court as "an artificial being, invisible, intangible and existing only in contemplation of the law." Think of it as a distinct and independent entity that exists separate from its owners.

Limited liability

The owners are not personally liable for debts and obligations of the corporation. They can personally lose only to the extent of their investment in the corporation, with the exception that they may be personally liable for certain types of taxes, such as payroll taxes withheld from the employees' paychecks but not paid to the Internal Revenue Service and state tax authorities. If the business fails or loses a lawsuit, the general creditors cannot attach the owners' homes, cars and other personal property.

note

Limited liability is one major reason so many businesses are incorporated.

Transferable interests

A corporation has the ability to raise capital by issuing shares of stock, whether public or private. Although the sale of public stock is highly regulated by both federal and state governments, ownership interest or shares of stock may be freely transferred to another party under the rules of the stockholder agreement. Once the interest is transferred, the new owner has all the rights and privileges associated with the former owner's interest. The Federal Trade Commission sets strict rules for issuing and publicly trading shares.

Tax deductions

The IRS allows corporate owners to fully deduct certain fringe benefits, such as pensions, retirement plans and other profit sharing plans, if properly documented.

Continuous life

Unlike a partnership or sole proprietorship, a corporation has a life independent of its owners and may continue to exist despite the death or incapacity of any or all of its directors.

Forming a corporation involves five major drawbacks:

1) *Double taxation.* A corporation generates its own profit, and is thus taxed separately from its members. Owners are also taxed on an individual basis, meaning a corporation is subject to "double taxation." (This may be avoided with a "subchapter S" corporation.)

2) *Bureaucracy and governmental regulation.* In order for the IRS to recognize a corporation as a separate entity, its directors must abide by strict regulations that govern corporate activity. Without well-maintained corporate records, the courts may disregard your corporate status and allow creditors to sue you personally for business debts. This is called "piercing the corporate veil," and happens more often than you think. States require you to file your Articles of Incorporation and sometimes bylaws. But to safely protect your corporate status, you must dutifully record all your meetings, resolutions and amendments. You must also inform the Secretary of State of any other changes involving your directors, registered agent, location or corporate purpose.

If the IRS audits your corporation and questions your salary or expenses, you must be able to prove company directors formally approved the action through well-documented corporate resolutions.

3) *Corporations are the most expensive* form of business to organize.

4) *Operating across state lines can be complicated* because corporations need to "qualify to do business" in states where they are not incorporated.

5) *Ending the corporate existence*, and in many cases even changing the structure of the organization, can be more complicated and costly than for other business entities.

The S corporation

DEFINITION

Once you have incorporated, you have the option of filing taxes under IRS Subchapter S. An *S corporation*, as this is called, has the corporate structure of a C or regular corporation but enjoys the same "pass through" tax status as a partnership, sole proprietorship or LLC. This means the S corporation itself avoids "double taxation," paying no federal taxes. There are

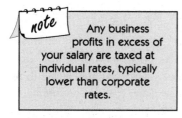

note Any business profits in excess of your salary are taxed at individual rates, typically lower than corporate rates.

a few things to remember, though. Your salary must be included on the payroll and is subject to employment taxes. Health benefits are not fully deductible as in a C corporation. However, an S corporation is allowed to "carry back" losses from prior years to offset current earnings.

The limited liability company

DEFINITION

To some business analysts, the *limited liability company (LLC)* represents the "best of both worlds." First, it offers the pass-through tax status of a partnership. Members are taxed on an individual basis; the company itself pays no taxes (unlike a corporation). Second, members also enjoy limited liability protection. Risk is limited to their business investment; personal assets are not subject to seizure from the company's creditors. Both advantages come with relatively few structural and paperwork requirements.

An IRS ruling in 1988 granted LLCs this special pass-through tax status. To qualify, organizations must exhibit no more than two of the following four corporate characteristics:

1) **Continuous life.** Prevent your LLC from existing as "a separate entity" in two simple steps. Specify a dissolution date, typically 30 years, in your Operating Agreement. Also, include a special directive written in the document that allows your company to continue to exist following any member's death, resignation, expulsion, bankruptcy or retirement without amending the Operating Agreement.

2) **Centralized management.** While corporations typically appoint a board of directors as management, an LLC must vest management power in its members to maintain pass-through status. Although one-member LLCs may have difficulty obtaining partnership tax status, husband and wife are recognized as separate members.

3) **Limited liability.** This one is pretty much a given, since it is a central reason for forming an LLC.

4) **Free transferability of interests.** Members may assign or transfer interests to a third party or creditor, who are entitled to receive dividends but are not allowed to vote without membership consent.

Most states require LLCs to register their Articles of Organization (similar to corporate Articles of Incorporation), the Operating Agreement (similar to corporate bylaws or a partnership agreement), and pay a fee. Check with your Secretary of State for statutes that may apply to you.

note

Few states require LLCs to keep records for major company actions.

The disadvantages of operating as an LLC include the lack of widespread familiarity and thus, acceptance of this type organization. IRS rules governing insolvency may create problems for the owners of the LLC. LLCs do not enjoy the advantages of IRS rulings when there is a sale of worthless stock or stock is sold at a loss. The sale of 50 percent or more of the ownership of the LLC in any 12-month period ends any tax advantage the company may have had with the IRS. And, LLCs may not engage in tax-free reorganizations.

Other asset protection strategies

Forming a corporation, limited partnership, or LLC is only the beginning. To arm yourself against a siege of potential disasters, explore a full array of asset protection strategies. Few entrepreneurs understand the advantage of forming multiple entities to build a defensive firewall that protects profit-making divisions from potential trouble spots. Separate entities can hold title to valuable assets including real estate and intellectual property such as trade secrets, patents, trademarks and copyrights. Other strategies can protect vital property such as mortgages and leases. A good start is to read E-Z Legal's *Asset Protection Made E-Z*.

What's in a name?

One of your first decisions is name selection—the name on your front door, in the phone book and on your company checks. Unless you are using your full name and operating as a sole proprietorship or general partnership, you must fill out a DBA (doing business as) form with the state in which you will be operating. Called a Fictitious Name in some states, this document is filed along with your corporation, limited partnership or LLC forms and reserves your name in that state.

An ideal name should:

- describe your business but not limit it to specifics. Phil's Fish & Chips attracts interest. But if he wants to broaden his menu and sell steaks, Phil may have to fill out another DBA and re-register his company in order to change the name to Phil's Eats.

- be easy to say, spell and remember. Simplicity sells, while tongue twisters are gnarled in failure.

- fit the character and clientele of your enterprise. "Dollar Craze" is more apropos than "Indubitably a Dollar."

- be composed of an acronym if you plan to use several words, i.e. Carmine's Auto Repair Service (CARS)

Use your name or a derivative if you have a good reputation in the community and want your business to be identified with you.

- start with a letter early in the alphabet if you depend on business from the yellow pages. Customers with no preference start with "A" and work their way towards "Z".

- never start with an article. Don't risk being listed under "A" or "The."

- be clever but not corny or deliberately misspelled. You may think "Kozy Kids Korner" is cute, but potential customers may look for you in the phone book under "C."

Look in phone books to see if the name has been taken. Check the Federal Trademark Registry as well as state registries to make sure no other company has exclusive federal or state trademark rights to the name. You can do a preliminary search on the Internet for a nominal fee. Access Trademark Scan through CompuServe or call them at (800) 421-7881. Attorneys generally charge between $50 and $500 to do such a search. If the name you use is deceptively similar to a trademarked name or one already in use, you may eventually be forced to give up the name or face a lawsuit.

Solicit suggestions from potential customers and clients, along with family and friends. Test your ideas on them, and try to develop a slogan or logo.

The
Marketing
Plan

Chapter 4

The Marketing Plan

What you'll find in this chapter:

➡ Marketing strategies

➡ Targeting your customers

➡ Image and advertising

➡ Making every penny count

➡ Taking advantage of the Internet

The secret to marketing is simple: define your niche and find ways to reach your target market. Putting principles into practice is complex. Many companies make the mistake of trying to be "all things to all people," but in doing so, they lack identity and sacrifice efficiency.

The focus of your marketing plan should be: "What can we do better than anyone, and how can we fully exploit this advantage?" This is called "positioning," or exploiting your "selling points." Your sights will narrow as you begin to analyze your relationship between customers and competitors.

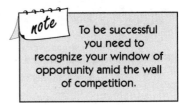

note To be successful you need to recognize your window of opportunity amid the wall of competition.

Marketing strategies

Marketing Steps

- Classifying Your Customers' Needs

- Targeting Your Customer(s)

- Examining Your "Niche"

- Identifying Your Competitors

- Assessing and Managing Your Available Resources
    - Financial
    - Human
    - Material
    - Production

Marketing Positioning

- Follower versus Leader

- Quality versus Price

- Innovator versus Adaptor

- Customer versus Product

- International versus Domestic

- Private Sector versus Government

Sales Strategy

- Use customer-oriented selling approach by constructing agreement

  Phase One: Establish rapport with customer by agreeing to discuss what the customer wants to achieve.

  Phase Two: Determine customer objective and situational factors by acknowledging what the customer wants to achieve and factors in the environment that influence these results.

  Your sales maxim should be: "Unless the proposition appeals to their INTEREST, unless it satisfies their DESIRES, and unless it shows them a GAIN" then they will not buy!"

  Phase Three: Recommend a customer action plan by agreeing that using your product/service will indeed achieve what customer wants.

  Phase Four: Obtain customer commitment by agreeing that the customer will acquire your product/service.

- Emphasize Customer Advantage

  Must be Read: When a competitive advantage cannot be demonstrated, it will not translate into a benefit.

  Must be Important to the Customer: When the competitive advantage varies between supplier and customer, the customer wins.

  Must be Specific: When a competitive advantage lacks specificity, it translates into mere puffery and is ignored.

  Must be Promotable: When a competitive advantage is proven, it is essential that your customer know it, lest it not exist at all.

Business Start-ups Made E-Z

Benefits vs. Features

- The six "O's" of organizing Customer Buying Behavior

ORIGINS of purchase:	Who buys it?
OBJECTIVES of purchase:	What do they need/buy?
OCCASIONS of purchase:	When do they buy it?
OUTLETS of purchase:	Where do they buy it?
OBJECTIVES of purchase:	Why do they buy it?
OPERATIONS of purchase:	How do they buy it?

- Convert features to benefits using the "...Which Means..."Transition

Features	"Which Means"	Benefits
Performance		Time Saved
Reputation		Reduced Cost
Components		Prestige
Colors		Bigger Savings
Sizes		Greater Profits
Exclusive		Greater Convenience
Uses		Uniform Production
Applications		Uniform Accuracy
Ruggedness		Continuous Output
Delivery		Leadership
Service		Increased Sales
Price		Economy of Use
Design		Ease of Use
Availability		Reduced Inventory
Installation		Low Operating Cost
Promotion		Simplicity
Lab Tests		Reduced Upkeep
Terms		Reduced Waste
Workmanship		Long Life

- Quality Customer Leads:

Level of need	Ability to pay
Authority to pay	Accessibility
Sympathetic attitude	Business history
One-source buyer	Reputation (price or quality buyer)

- Buying Motives:

Rational	Emotional
Economy of Purchase	Pride of Appearance
Economy of Use	Pride of Ownership
Efficient Profits	Desire of Prestige
Increased Profits	Desire for Recognition
Durability	Desire to Imitate
	Accurate Performance
	Desire for Variety
	Labor-Saving
	Safety
	Time-Saving
	Curiosity
	Simple Construction
Desire to Create	Desire to Be Unique
Simple Operation	Desire for Security
Ease of Repair	Convenience
Ease of Installation	Space-Saving

> **E-Z TIP**
> Try to draw conclusions about the lifestyle, beliefs, hobbies, habits and spending patterns that will lead people to your business.

Target customers

Profile every aspect of the type of people who may need—and buy—your product. Start with basic demographics: age, gender, income, occupation and residence. Factors that influence a customer's choice typically extend well beyond the basics. How large of a customer base do you project? In what areas can you expand your market? What factors will influence their decisions? Is the market segmented according to location, price, quality, selection or service?

Analyze the competition

List the names and addresses of your five nearest direct competitors. Supply as much relevant information about them as you can. Compare their operations to yours in the same way you described your company in the previous section. How long have they been in business? How many people do they employ? What are their respective market shares? Are they prospering, growing or faltering? How do their products and services differ from yours? What are their marketing strategies, strengths and weaknesses? What ideas will you borrow from them and how do you plan to achieve a competitive edge?

What price is right?

While customers, competition and industry standards provide a "ballpark" index, the price you charge for products and services is entirely up to you. Plenty of start-up companies believe offering the lowest price in town will draw the most customers and thus spell success. However, they

While a competitive price may attract some customers, a lower price tag may also drive down the "perceived value" of your products.

overlook the No. 1 priority: making profits. Smaller businesses rarely receive large volume discounts like their larger competitors. Thus, low price coupled with increased variable costs such as materials, labor and taxes simply means less gross profit per sale.

Your pricing should strike a balance between your net profit and your market share to optimize total profits. Capitalize on current market conditions and dominate market share by being the pricing aggressor, rather than follower. Ask yourself: "What are my customers willing to pay?"

More promotion for less

How will customers find out about your new enterprise? An essential cog in any start-up machine is a strong promotional engine. Effective marketing means reaching your target audience with a message that grabs attention and calls them to action.

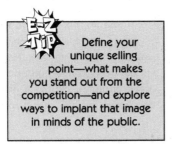

Define your unique selling point—what makes you stand out from the competition—and explore ways to implant that image in minds of the public.

Select media that reaches your customers most efficiently. Television, radio and newspaper ads reach the mainstream, but are often too expensive for small start-ups. Consider flyers, direct mail and billboards. Promotion can be as simple as placing your work number on company vehicle or as unusual as an airplane message. Commit to your marketing campaign as a long-term investment, one that requires patience to pay dividends. Base your marketing budget on a percentage of sales, and closely monitor its cost-effectiveness.

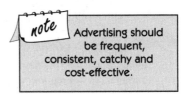

note Advertising should be frequent, consistent, catchy and cost-effective.

Image is everything

Good marketing starts with your overall appearance. *First impressions are lasting ones.* Be prepared when you open, with sparkling floors and full shelves. Neatness counts, as does the tone of your voice and the smile on your face. The more professional you appear, the more respect you earn.

A signature logo on your storefront sign, letterhead and business cards can build your identity. Producing a quality brochure requires more detail. It should include a detailed description of your company, its products and services, testimonials from satisfied customers, pictures that add to your message, and ordering information.

A print shop may be able to develop the image you're looking for, or you could hire a freelance graphic artist. Most local college art students will work inexpensively.

If you are not adept at writing and design, hire a creative person and explain in detail how the brochure will be used (point-of-purchase, trade shows, mailings, etc.) and what it should convey. They will help you pick sizes, paper, ink and other factors that influence cost.

Free publicity

Often you can grab media attention by sending a simple letter to local newspapers and radio stations, local and cable television, trade publications and magazines. Explain your new business, why it is unique and how the public would benefit from hearing about it. Try to give your story a hook—an intriguing twist a reporter can focus on—and be prepared to answer questions with quotable lines. Include photographs and other helpful promotional material. If your story is featured, be prepared to field a potential blitz of inquiries and orders. Laminate the clipping to display near your front door and make photocopies for mailings.

The best advertising is often word of mouth recommendation. Quality products and friendly service speak for themselves, and will get your satisfied customers talking. Encourage customers to spread the word. It can be as simple as a saying, "Be sure to mention us to a friend." Use the phrase as a sign inside the door, behind your sales counter, or print it on the receipt. You could also offer a discount for bringing in new customers or an incentive for frequent visits.

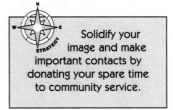

Solidify your image and make important contacts by donating your spare time to community service.

Make every penny count

Large corporations spend millions on television ads that have little impact on sales. These soft-sell campaigns work to etch a corporate identity into the minds of the masses. Small start-up companies don't have that luxury. So how can you get the most bang for your advertising buck? Here are some tips:

- *Frequency outdoes fancy.* Classifieds and small ads in newspapers, magazines and phone books that accurately target your customers are inexpensive and efficient. Steady repetition helps the public remember your name.

- *Look before you leap.* Be skeptical of unsolicited advertising that will inevitably bombard your new businesses. Before buying into the hype, investigate the source and demand proof of results.

- *Negotiate.* The price of advertising time and space is never set in stone. If it's not sold, the opportunity is lost. Don't always settle for the standard rate.

- **Save commission.** Agencies receive a 15 percent commission to place ads. If you know where and when you want your ad to run, you can save commission by placing the ad yourself.

- **Limit risk.** Some magazines, television and radio stations offer no-risk advertising agreements in which you pay only commission on the number of responses generated. Examples are PI (per inquiry) and PO (per order).

- **Reserve remnant space.** If you want to advertise in regional editions of magazines, you can cut the cost in half with a "stand-by" arrangement. Notify the publication well in advance, and when space is available, your ad goes in.

- **Make your mark.** Many good marketing ideas are not created—they are copied. Find out what is working for your competitors, then put an original new twist on their idea.

- **Co-op advertising.** If you sell products from a known national supplier, ask the supplier to contribute to the cost of the ad and mention them in your ad. The advantages can be twofold: They may provide added funds for promoting their product and add credibility to your company.

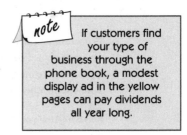

note   If customers find your type of business through the phone book, a modest display ad in the yellow pages can pay dividends all year long.

- **Barter is better.** See if you can work out a trade of your products or services for advertising.

Don't get lost in cyberspace

How fast is the Internet catching on? Consider these startling facts:

- more Americans are buying computers than TVs

- one-third of U.S. adults use the Internet

- users average 10 hours per week online

Millions of U.S. businesses have created commercial sites touting their goods and services to potential Web customers, but many sites lack direction and become quickly forgotten amid the competition. An effective site can be a boon to any size business. It can attract interest, assist customers, produce profit, expand distribution and reduce expenses. Some tips:

◆ *Your site must be easy to find.* Registering "key words" with various search engines will help direct searches to your site. Incorporate your site's address, or URL, on all promotional and packaging materials.

◆ *Your site also must be speedy and simple to navigate.* Supply information your customers need in a practical yet dynamic way.

◆ *Encourage feedback through surveys, and respond quickly to your customers' needs.* Or provide faster service and access to more detailed information with a Frequently-Asked Questions (FAQs) page. Give links to other helpful or interesting sites, and have these sites reciprocate. Promote return visits by updating frequently and offering freebies and contests. Keep track of traffic statistics and visitor data, adjusting content—and your budget—accordingly.

> **note** Your web site should be more than a static company brochure; ideally, it should entertain and interact with visitors, treating them as individuals rather than numbers.

♦ *Open an online storefront or product catalog* and expand your potential market from local to global—overnight. With improved security measures, online credit card transactions are becoming as accepted as ATM cards. By 2000, experts predict e-commerce will bring in billions, largely from products under $50.

♦ *Today companies of all sizes rely on productivity software* to automate accounting, shipping and even inventory. Tomorrow's technical innovations will make it just as easy to integrate your online storefront with all your internal operations, further streamlining your business and strengthening your competitive edge.

> **E-Z TIP**
>
> Making your products and services downloadable over the Internet can not only widen your distribution channels, but it will also cut printing, packaging, delivery, material, labor and retail costs—savings you can pass on to your customers.

 Preparing for the future is vital to your success. Companies failing to fully exploit opportunities along the Information Superhighway will be left behind.

Service with a smile

One important marketing advantage a small company possesses is personalized customer service. Follow these eight rules:

1) Train employees to be courteous, professional and informed.

2) Establish procedures for handling customer complaints and returns, rehearsing solutions before problems occur.

3) Make yourself available to resolve the more serious conflicts.

4) Provide comment cards or a suggestion box and respond quickly to concerns.

5) Avoid false or misleading advertising claims.

6) Set high-quality standards for suppliers, and make it a point you refuse to sell defective or dangerous products.

7) Honor all guarantees and warranties, clearly stating terms and conditions.

8) Join a consumer advocacy group. This will show you are committed to serving your customer's needs and establishes valuable credibility.

The Financial Plan

Chapter 5

The Financial Plan

What you'll find in this chapter:

➠ Strengthening your credit

➠ Your start-up costs

➠ Cash flow

➠ Income and growth projections

➠ The financial documents you need

How do you get money for your business? Naysayers who shy away from pursuing their own venture say, "You need money to make money." That's only partly true. You do need to invest some money, but not necessarily your money. Thousands of prosperous entrepreneurs started out small with little or no money down and grew to become industry leaders.

Repair and bolster your credit

Before you start looking for loans, take the time to repair and bolster your credit history. Start by paying off all outstanding debts, and closing inactive accounts. Repair any marks at least three months in advance of applying for a loan. E-Z Legal's *Credit Repair Made E-Z* is ideal for this purpose.

Request a report from the major credit agencies. These companies handle literally millions of reports each year and mistakes are common. They report all records of loan notes, partial payments, liens, bankruptcies, late payments, wage attachments and more. If you find inaccuracies in your report, write a letter to the agency challenging the accuracy of the item. By federal law, the credit bureau must verify that item within 30 days or remove it from your credit report. You may challenge a negative item for any reason. Some common reasons are:

- it is older than seven years

- the company that reported the negative item to the credit bureau is no longer in business

If you need to establish credit, take advantage of credit card companies that offer cards to businesses.

- it contains a wrong account number or name

- the incident never occurred and the bureau is confusing you with someone else

note

Creditors also look at how much credit has been extended to you. A home mortgage or auto loan with proven payments shows financial responsibility. Even a short-term loan for a holiday, vacation or home improvement, if paid off, helps supplement a record otherwise listing only credit cards.

Work the numbers

No business plan is complete without thoroughly analyzing the numbers. Your financial plan must address the following areas:

start-up costs	personal financial statements
income statements	cash flow statements
break even analysis	growth projections

Start-up costs

Although some rush into business with the philosophy, "the more you spend, the more you make," companies that start out "lean and mean," learning the value of a buck through tight money management, are better off. Aim for a start-up venture that is small enough to be financed while still large enough to be successful.

Cash flow and income projections

How much capital will you need to finance your start-up? This can be difficult to judge, especially before you have a few months' figures to rely on. To ensure you always have enough cash on hand, your projections need to be as accurate as possible.

For projected expenses, begin with fixed costs, including rent, utilities, insurance, equipment and salary. Add variable costs, such as inventory, supplies, production costs and delivery. For projected income, use industry standards and demographic analysis to project how many customers you will draw. Estimate the average price customers will spend on your goods. Take into account the impact of major competitors, the scope of your promotional efforts and the attractiveness of your location. Subtract a quarter of your modest income estimate as it inevitably takes time to develop customer awareness and loyalty. If expenses outweigh income, you need to rework your plan in order to cut expenses, obtain a loan or conduct a sales promotion to increase income.

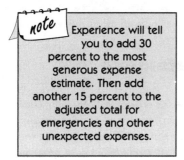

note Experience will tell you to add 30 percent to the most generous expense estimate. Then add another 15 percent to the adjusted total for emergencies and other unexpected expenses.

DEFINITION A major factor in your financing is *liquidity*, or the ability to pay your bills. Liquid assets include cash and possessions that can readily be turned into cash, such as checks, credit receivables and inventory—some more easily than others. Will you have enough liquid assets to cover all impending bills? To be solvent, you must be able to pay your bills as they fall due. Your assets must exceed your liabilities. The ratio should be at least 2-to-1; 3- or 4-to-1 is safer. A sound practice in the early going is to add cash and other assets to your company while cutting expenses such as your personal salary.

Personal financial statements

Most lenders require you to project your salary as part of overall expenses. If you agree to a low salary, it proves your willingness to sacrifice immediate personal gain to ensure a profitable venture—especially if you sacrificed a lucrative career to do so. Include with your fiscal projections a record of your personal finances, and list each asset you will contribute along with the market value of each.

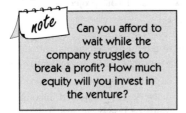
note Can you afford to wait while the company struggles to break a profit? How much equity will you invest in the venture?

Profit & Loss Statement

Complete monthly and yearly Profit & Loss Statements by combining expense and income ledgers. Under income, leave out sales tax and "non-business income." Subtract net inventory used (amount you started with plus purchases made minus current stock) to determine your gross profit. Subtract all other "operating expenses," except sales tax and any "non-deductible" expenses, and you discover your magic number: net profit. Refer to your accounting ledgers and Profit & Loss Statements frequently to find trends, such as slow sales cycles, over-spending and stock shrinkage, you need to account for to survive.

Break even point

How much in sales will you need to make profit? Break-even analysis, as it is called, is used to determine how soon your income will cover your start-up costs.

You can also gauge the sales thrust necessary to make new products viable. Take total fixed costs (rent, utilities, insurance, etc.). Divide this by unit selling price minus variable cost per unit (supplies, labor, marketing, etc.). Higher net profit means fewer items you need to sell (see What price is right?).

$$\frac{\text{Total fixed costs}}{\text{Unit selling price} - \text{variable unit cost}} = \text{Break-even Point}$$

Growth projections

Lenders like to see the potential for growth in their investment. What areas for growth do you see in your industry? Do you plan to enter new markets or expand your product line? How much do you plan to invest in research and development? What share of the market will you command in the future.

Outline a sensible five-year forecast with numbers to accurately support your beliefs.

Financial Documents

To obtain a loan, you will be required to furnish some or all of the following documents:

◆ **Financial Data**

1) Loan application(s)

2) Capital equipment and supply list

3) Balance sheet

4) Break-even analysis

5) Pro-forma (anticipated) income projections (profit & loss statements)

- three-year summary

- detail by month, first year

- detail by quarters, second and third years

- assumptions upon which projections were based

6) Pro-forma (anticipated) cash flow (Follow guidelines for 5)

◆ **Supporting Documents**

1) Tax returns of principals for last three years

2) Personal financial statement (all banks have these forms)

3) In the case of a franchised business, a copy of franchise contract and all supporting documents provided by the franchisor

4) Copy of proposed lease or purchase agreement for building space

5) Copy of licenses and other legal documents

6) Copy of resumes of all principals

7) Copies of letters of intent from suppliers, etc.

Financing your business

Chapter 6

Financing your business

Finance whenever possible

Your goal should be to finance your start-up with as little of your own money down as possible. That way you have money in reserve in case you underestimated your costs or need it in an emergency. Interest on most business loans is tax-deductible. Why not accept "free money" subsidized by Uncle Sam? Thousands of penniless entrepreneurs have started successful ventures with nothing more than a solid plan, marketing expertise and a long line of financiers. Leverage allows you to build your business today so it can stand its own two feet tomorrow.

When shopping for credit, aim for the longest terms, lowest interest rate, and the least collateral and personal liability as possible. You may choose fixed, lump sum, periodic or balloon payments. Prioritize them according to your specific needs. In the financing section of your business plan be sure to detail the interest rate, terms and conditions you desire. Carefully plan your cash flow statement as accurately as possible. Negotiate payments to coincide with both short and long term income projections. This requires planning and discipline. Worst-case

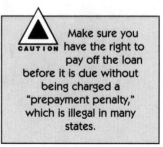

Make sure you have the right to pay off the loan before it is due without being charged a "prepayment penalty," which is illegal in many states.

cash flow scenarios are safer and more realistic. What is the least amount of money you will make? Time the opening of your company for approximately a month before peak season. Promote your venture well in advance.

So where can you obtain money? Start with family, friends, business associates, suppliers (see "Innovative Financing") and retailers. Typically those

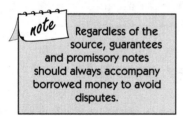

Regardless of the source, guarantees and promissory notes should always accompany borrowed money to avoid disputes.

most familiar with you and your business are most willing to back you. Be sure to get all terms and conditions in writing. A promissory note outlines the interest, payment plan, terms and conditions of the loan. Sign the original and mark "Copy" on the duplicate you file.

Two other traditional sources of loans are commercial banks and the Small Business Association.

Bank loans

You should approach a commercial bank for a loan only after exhausting all other resources. Typical commercial loans from a bank provide working capital and carry five-year payback terms with higher interest rates than personal loans. Most states have a limit on the interest rate a bank is allowed to charge on business loans. If you can get it, a line of credit is ideal for covering unexpected expenses as they occur.

While most banks are reluctant to lend to a start-up, you may be able to find a progressive bank known to back small businesses. Like a lot of business transactions, bank loans often hinge on a personal relationship with a loan officer. Let him know you are trustworthy professional with a solid business plan, rather than a desperate soul searching for a helping hand. Take him on a tour your facilities; share your ideas over dinner or a round of golf. Social contacts can make quality character references.

Typical institutional lenders invest no more than 50 percent of needed financing, expecting you to cover the rest through personal contributions or some other sources. A substantial personal investment proves your commitment to the venture. The bank will likely put a lien on your company's receivables, inventory and owned equipment. Be careful when pledging personal assets to secure your loan. If your business falters, you may have trouble recovering enough to try again. Even if you form a corporation, the bank may still sue you for non-pledged assets and garnish your wages in order to recover the principal. A loan to an LLC may require a personal guarantee, which also binds shareholders during the start-up stages.

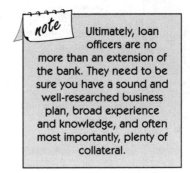

Ultimately, loan officers are no more than an extension of the bank. They need to be sure you have a sound and well-researched business plan, broad experience and knowledge, and often most importantly, plenty of collateral.

Pinpoint how large a loan you need with an itemized list of accurately projected up-front expenses, typically for the first 16 months. Asking for slightly more than you need gives you a comfortable cushion. But expenses of more than 15 percent in excess of comparable businesses in your area looks suspicious to any intelligent loan officer. If you can establish a line of credit, your company gains access to money whenever needed.

SBA loans

If you are turned down by at least one bank, you may qualify for a loan from the Small Business Association. This federal government bureaucracy has backed over $29 billion in loans to 200,000 small businesses. The SBA may either guarantee a percent of an institutional loan, or loan you the money directly. If approved for the LowDoc program, named so for its short one-page application, a bank may loan you up to $100,000 backed by a 90 percent SBA guarantee. The Micro Loan program offers up to $25,000 for women and minority entrepreneurs and businesses in low-income areas. Other SBA loan programs offer up to $500,000 but require you to show profit for two years, work full-time in the business and pledge collateral. However, in some cases a solid plan and proven management skills may get you approved.

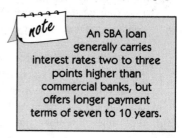

An SBA loan generally carries interest rates two to three points higher than commercial banks, but offers longer payment terms of seven to 10 years.

To be eligible for SBA assistance, you must fit their quite-liberal description of a "small business." Though they fluctuate by industry, three very general standards are:

- manufacturers with fewer than 500 employees

- service and retail businesses with annual revenues of $3.5 million or less

- wholesalers with no more than 100 employees

For information on how to contact the SBA, see the Resources section of this guide.

Buying a business

Chapter 7
Buying a business

What you'll find in this chapter:

➠ When you want to purchase a business
➠ Questions to ask before buying
➠ Buying an existing business
➠ Getting appraisals
➠ Buying a franchise

Perhaps you are considering buying an existing business or a franchise. Both options frequently provide their own financing to go with an established business plan.

Buying a business

When you purchase a business, you buy its assets including equipment, supplies, customer list, inventory and lease, plus intellectual property such as patents, trademarks, trade secrets and copyrights. You may also assume its liabilities including debts and other legal obligations such as warranties, employee contracts and benefits. You may be able to negotiate favorable payment terms directly from the owner such as low down payment, below-market interest rate, and lengthy payoffs.

Before you invest your first penny, thoroughly investigate every aspect of the business. Ask yourself these three sets of questions:

1) How much is the business worth? Is the market growing or shrinking? Is new competition sprouting up? Why is the owner selling? Use the same evaluation process as though you were starting a new business.

2) What advantages will you have over the previous owner? Can you exhibit more expertise or knowledge of your market? Will you be able to keep all current accounts and suppliers?

3) How easily can you transfer the business into your name? Will new zoning laws apply to a new owner? Can you transfer the lease? Inspect all lease papers, supplier agreements and financial records.

As in buying a home, an appraisal is essential. See the Resources section of this guide for how to find an appraiser.

Franchises

DEFINITION

Restaurants, hotels and gas stations are common *franchise* businesses. These businesses are part of a regional or national chain but are owned and operated by local individuals. The franchisor sells its nationally recognized trademark name, its successful business plan, and often its expert guidance—from picking a location to marketing, from managing personnel to accounting systems and day-to-day operations. In return, the franchisee pays up-front franchise fees plus royalties, or a percentage of income typically from gross sales. In

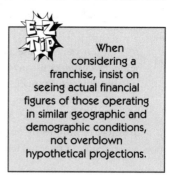

When considering a franchise, insist on seeing actual financial figures of those operating in similar geographic and demographic conditions, not overblown hypothetical projections.

addition, the franchisee buys equipment, inventory and supplies direct from parent company along with training fees and a percentage of co-op advertising.

Ideally, this bureaucratic control leads to efficiency of scale. But often owning a franchise is very restrictive, allowing for little input for adapting to local conditions. Learn what you can expect from the parent company in terms of marketing, financial and operational assistance. Get all promises in writing. Talk to other franchisees and find out their problems, solutions and benefits.

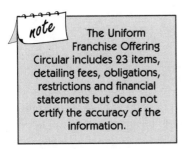

note The Uniform Franchise Offering Circular includes 23 items, detailing fees, obligations, restrictions and financial statements but does not certify the accuracy of the information.

The Federal Trade Commission requires all franchisors to issue prospective franchisee owners two documents that disclose full details of the arrangement: an offering circular and a franchising agreement. While not required, the Uniform Franchise Offering Circular, prepared by the North American Securities Administrators Association, is used by most franchisors. As for the franchising agreement, terms may or may not be negotiable, depending on the size and stature of the franchisor.

The Operational Plan

Chapter 8

The Operational Plan

What you'll find in this chapter:

➡ Where to locate your business

➡ Different industries available to you

➡ The home-based business

➡ Inventory and expenses

➡ Licenses and other legalities

Orchestrating a small business start-up involves coordinating a broad range of decisions at once. You must select an affordable yet effective location, obtain ample supplies, equipment and inventory, hire and manage a cohesive staff, and deal with countless legal and financial issues. Such a flood of responsibilities demands a diligent, organized, resourceful person.

Location, location, location

Choosing a location may be one of the most important business decisions, and biggest investments, you'll make. Dedicate plenty of time, patience and persistence to find a site that will offer you the greatest benefits. The majority of small businesses will move or go under within five years. This means you don't always have to look for vacancies. Find a desirable location and inquire when the lease expires. Ask around; you might discover an attractive place before it gets listed—and possibly at a better price. Involve a host of resources, including your city's Chamber of Commerce, bankers, engineers, contractors, plus your accountant and attorney. Also, find a consultant or real estate agent you can trust. The type of business you run and the customers you serve will answer your two basic questions:

1) How important is location?

2) How much space do you need?

The retail business

In retail, location can make or break you. With excellent promotion, you may be able to survive in a remote location if you offer specialty goods or high-ticket items such as furniture or automobiles. But businesses that depend on heavy foot traffic for impulse sales such as clothing, videos or convenience goods need to be located on a main artery. Neighboring stores should be compatible with yours. For example, gas stations and fast food chains are for people on the run; movie theaters draw leisurely crowds suited more for upscale restaurants.

An enclosed mall is the most fashionable, and potentially most profitable, place for a retail business. Boasting solid name recognition and credit ratings, chain stores dominate the scene and make it almost impossible for independents to compete for a lease. If you plan to rent space in a shopping center, adequate parking is a primary concern. Investigate its merchants' association. Make sure they keep the premises clean and well maintained. They may offer group advertising and

For a small, independent business, co-signers, lease insurance, kiosks and sublets can be your ticket into a shopping mall location.

insurance. Active organizations even lobby for local taxes to be applied toward new lighting, roads and sidewalks. Malls and shopping centers typically charge percentage of sales in addition to fixed base rent, restrict the number of competing businesses, and require you to be open during set hours of operation.

Often retailers rent a space with cinder walls and concrete floors. As renovation costs go through the roof, they become saddled with an astronomical construction bill that stifles their ability to maintain an attractive inventory. Months later they close their designer doors for good. Before you move in, discuss your needs with the landlord, who may be willing to contribute to the renovation costs in order to improve his property. Also, you may be able to work the costs into rent rather than pay a lump sum.

The manufacturing business

Industrial parks typically are situated near bus routes, highways, railroads and airports, providing convenient mass transportation of both goods and

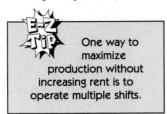

laborers. They also provide ample parking and easy-access dock space. Spacious facilities are available at bargain prices in low-grade urban areas or in vast rural environs. In the latter case, be certain there are there enough workers nearby.

The service business

Professional service providers (doctors, lawyers and consultants) are one sector that benefits from a "status location." But plenty of enterprises are adapting to less glamorous environs and prospering. Thousands of thrifty entrepreneurs operate service and mail order businesses from their garage or spare bedroom, keeping overhead to a minimum. Working from home saves you rent, eliminates travel time and cost, and allows you to deduct from your taxes the percentage of your residence you use for business. It also allows more flexible hours, more time to spend with your family and less time in traffic. Make sure zoning in your neighborhood does not prohibit working from your home. Other bargain locations include older homes, boarded-up stores and basement space below other retailers.

Negotiating a lease

Business owners are often anxious to lock in a long-term lease on a prime location, because commercial lease terms are typically four to 10 years

A sublease with a shorter duration is a wise choice for a start-up, if you can negotiate it.

or five years with an option to rent for another five years. However, after their business has settled, they sometimes realize they either can't afford the rent or need more space long before their lease is up for renewal.

In some cases, it is not the tenant who is at fault but the landlord. Insert a clause protecting your rights to the location should the owner go broke. As with all legal matters, make sure all agreements with your landlord are in writing. Specify rental costs and who pays for utilities and services such as cleaning, landscaping and snow removal. Look over the sample Commercial Lease (Form B-06) to familiarize yourself with common lease clauses. Also consider inserting a purchase option, which allows you to buy the property after a specified period of time.

If your landlord has confidence in your business plan, and if you put up collateral or are willing to pledge your personal guarantee, you may be able to negotiate a lease on credit. This allows you to defer the security deposit and the first few months' advance rent payments until your business begins generating income. You also may try to negotiate a flexible rent based on the traffic your business experiences.

Here are a few other considerations:

- Is there ample parking for customers and employees?

- Is commerce affected by seasonal trends?

- Is the area clean, safe and brightly lit at night?

- Does the building comply with industry and government safety requirements?

- How much will you pay for utilities, insurance and renovation?

The home-based business

Working out of the home has become a significant and growing phenomenon in the United States. Home-based business owners are self-employed individuals who operate a business or profession primarily from or in a home office. *Telecommuters* are employees who do office work at home during normal business hours.

DEFINITION

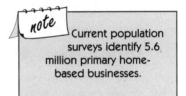
Current population surveys identify 5.6 million primary home-based businesses.

The Characteristics of Business Owners survey found that more than 7 million businesses—including the majority of businesses owned by women (54.6 percent) and nearly half of all non-minority businesses owned by men (49.8 percent)—were home-based. It has been estimated that there are 10.4 million home business owners—including those with a side business—and 9.5 million freelance workers, totaling 19.9 million "home-based business" persons out of a work force of 122.7 million.

Owning a home-based business and working at home for wages are both labor market options that offer flexibility to potential entrepreneurs and employees. For many people, especially stay-at home parents, the home-based business is not only convenient but profitable.

The most important factor to remember when choosing to run a home-based business is the tax factor. Be certain to have your accountant or tax consultant advise you when setting up your home as an office, since the tax deductions involved in the division of house from office are complicated. Be certain to keep careful records of your house-as-office separate from your house-as-home.

Equipment, fixtures and inventory

DEFINITION

Your new business needs money for inventory and raw materials—known as *working capital* because it generates profit and makes your business work. Forget the fine marble desk, shiny new shelves and flashy company cars until profits are rolling in. Limit your fixed costs to things that are absolutely necessary to operate the business.

Innovative financing

Be creative in finding and financing furnishings and fixtures. Places to discover bargain fixtures include auctions, newspaper classifieds, trade publications, chain stores that are remodeling, and equipment supply firms who inherit unwanted items their new equipment replaces. Manufacturers are eager to finance used equipment just so they may be rid of it. They may offer warranties and service contracts, but beware of inflated finance charges. Leasing can be a smart option if equipment lasts less than five years, depreciates quickly or is a candidate for expensive repairs.

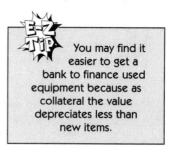

You may find it easier to get a bank to finance used equipment because as collateral the value depreciates less than new items.

Will you be using a major wholesaler, supplier or distributor? If so, they may be willing to not only furnish their raw materials on credit, but even subsidize your equipment for a few months of operation. They would hold title to the assets and lease them to your business until your purchases from them reach a pre-agreed dollar amount.

Consider sharing equipment with another business or contracting out your production altogether.

In retail, under-merchandising is more dangerous than over-stocking. Shoppers feel uncomfortable in a bare store, and you will never make enough profit to fill it. Consider a mix of related tie-in lines or substitutes as you begin to build. Some stores rent floor space to smaller retailers with complimentary goods. Have your accountant define your break-even point based on a realistic sales projection, then follow industry-standard inventory turnover figures.

Excess inventories can be equally damaging—limiting merchandising flexibility and responsiveness, cutting into cash reserves and forcing you to pay high interest rates. Always keep an eye on inventory, analyzing the delicate balance between supply and demand. Distinguish between hot sellers and slow-movers, keeping the optimal amount of each on hand.

Monitoring expenses

To eliminate shrinkage and overspending, administer tight control over all financial transactions. This involves an intricate yet organized system of checks and balances on invoices, inventory, receivables and payroll. Establish an amount, say $500,

Review, duplicate and keep safe all records for at least six years, and regularly audit and verify receivables.

above which purchases must be approved by a designated company officer.

note One expense you must monitor closely is your energy bill. Make sure your bill is not out of line with industry averages, readily available through the U.S. Department of Energy. Your utility company may conduct a free survey and suggest ways to help you operate more efficiently. Also, keep long distance phone bills in check. Restrict its use to business calls and hold employees accountable by assigning each a personal access number and reviewing bills monthly.

Business insurance

How much insurance you need depends on your business. Check with your landlord, lender and state. Your insurance agent may offer a comprehensive Business Owner's Policy (BOP) or an industry-specific policy, often available through trade associations. Which perils should you account for: fire, flood, wind, earthquake? Will coverage provide for replacement cost or current value? For older property replacement cost may be much higher.

 Shop around and read policies carefully so you are clear about specific coverage and deductibles.

Also find out what it takes to make a claim and how quickly it will be processed.

Most states require worker's compensation insurance for all employees. This provides benefits to workers injured or killed on the job regardless of fault. Premiums are based upon payroll and risk of occupation, and are tax-deductible. You may not be required to insure outside contractors, but it is a good idea to ask for their Certificate of Insurance before hiring. Uninsured contractors may hold you liable if they are injured while working for you. In most cases vehicle coverage is also required.

You will be required to insure expensive assets (buildings, equipment) you leased or bought on credit. Any facility accessible to customers or clients, plus all potentially dangerous products, should carry liability coverage. To keep premiums low, install sprinkler and security systems, conduct safety training and fire drills, and check drivers' records. Surety bonds, professional malpractice, extended coverage, employee theft, crime coverage, business interruption and bad debt insurance all are part of the mix.

 To compete for qualified employees, you may need to offer a variety of health insurance benefits. Pension plans, Keoghs and IRA accounts each carry an intricate web of terms and tax consequences. Expert advice from an unbiased agent can help you structure the coverage you need for the lowest price.

Licenses and other legalities

Numerous state and federal laws protect consumers from misleading advertising and labeling, as well as deceptive product guarantees and warranties. Many states require a license to conduct business by telephone or door-to-door, or to sell liquor, firearms, tobacco and lottery tickets. Local licenses sometimes strive to protect consumer interests and stimulate commerce, and at the same time raise revenues for city government.

Take advantage of small business assistance agencies which act as liaisons to translate government legalese, list licenses and permits that may apply to you, and help you comply with regulations.

Zoning ordinances apply to different areas of your city, restrict certain business activities such as water use, water and air quality, waste disposal, parking and signs. Contractors, landlords, business advocates and your city's chamber of commerce can help explain ordinances and help convince zoning board administrators your business will provide a valuable community service. With a little persistence, you may be able to negotiate re-zoning or obtain a variance. You must also comply with fire, police, health and building code regulations or face fines and penalties. Seek advice from colleagues, trade associations and government agencies.

Call your local Occupational Safety and Health Administration (OSHA) office for a free on-site safety consultation. An inspector will provide practical advice about to complying with government standards but usually won't report bad results or issue a citation unless a serious violation is evident.

Accounting and taxes

9

Chapter 9
Accounting and taxes

What you'll find in this chapter:

➡ Your financial records

➡ Bookkeeping ledgers

➡ Extending credit

➡ Credit cautions and alternatives

➡ Taxes and your business

Few entrepreneurs are trained accountants, but the successful ones let the numbers lead them. Before you devise marketing or financial strategies, or make most everyday decisions, always ask: "What's the bottom line?" Answers will surface if you maintain accurate and complete financial records.

Start by opening a separate checking account for your business with your company's name, address and phone number printed on the checks. To open a company bank account, you need to obtain an Employer Identification Number for your company. To obtain this, simply file Form SS-4 with the Internal Revenue Service. If you are a corporation, you may be required to produce a "corporate resolution" duly signed,

To keep good financial records, you don't need an accounting degree. You just need to be organized, diligent and accurate with addition calculations.

often with the corporate seal, as an official corporate indication of authorization to open such an account. Write checks for every business-related purchase, and deposit all income into your business checking account. Balance your account at least monthly, and keep all cancelled checks on file for at least three years—required for IRS tax audits. To keep track of expenditures, never write checks to "cash."

DEFINITION

The two basic accounting methods are *cash* and *accrual*. With the cash method, you record income at the time cash is received and record the expense when you make the payment. With the accrual method, you record a transaction at the time it is made regardless of when the payment occurs. The IRS requires you to declare the accounting method you will use and if your corporation's annual average gross receipts exceed $5 million you must use the accrual method. If you keep sales inventory it is generally preferable to use accrual accounting.

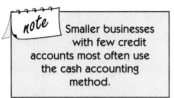

Smaller businesses with few credit accounts most often use the cash accounting method.

Bookkeeping Ledgers

Basic accounting involves the six ledgers included in this program: Income, Expense, Payroll, Inventory, Credit and Equipment Depreciation. Make an entry in the appropriate ledger for each transaction, including date, description and amount. Tally monthly and yearly totals, then store them in a safe, fireproof place.

Income Ledger

DEFINITION

For each ledger entry, you must distinguish between "business" and "non-business" income. *Business income* is money generated through the sale of products or services. *Non-business income* is raised by means unrelated to your business activity, such as a partner contribution, bank interest or loan repayment. Also distinguish between "taxable" and "non-taxable" sales, and record all sales tax collected. Sales volume determines how often you post income and what proof of purchase you use—either detailed cash register printouts or your suppliers' dated, numbered and signed invoices. Be sure to file voids and returns separately.

Expense

As important as how you earn money is how you spend it. For each purchase you make, obtain a copy of the invoice or receipt. Stamp "posted" on the invoice as you enter it in your ledger. Write the check number on each paid invoice and stamp it "paid." If you see a need to set aside "petty cash" for expenses too small to write a check, make out one check payable to "cash" for $20 to $50. Keep the cash in a safe place with an informal "slush fund ledger" that lists name, date, purpose and amount of each withdrawal.

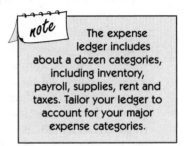

note The expense ledger includes about a dozen categories, including inventory, payroll, supplies, rent and taxes. Tailor your ledger to account for your major expense categories.

Payroll

Under the payroll category in the Expense Ledger, include net pay and withheld payroll taxes (at the time you pay them). Use a separate Payroll Ledger to break down all other detailed costs.

Inventory

Make sure you always have enough inventory on hand by keeping an accurate inventory ledger. This records the date and quantity of each order, how many have been sold, and how many are still in stock. You can keep an eye on such pivotal factors as which items are "slow movers" and how long it takes for your supplier to deliver. Today, many computer programs are available to eliminate the tedium and inaccuracy of manual inventory control.

Credit

You can keep track of credit accounts in one of two ways: use of a ledger or a multiple-copy invoice file. In either case, keep track of when payments are due, when they come in, and the outstanding balance.

Financial savvy

Many small businesses limit their accountant's duties to preparing quarterly and year-end taxes. But without regular budgets, cash flow statements, expense cost analyses and other navigational numbers, these accountants lack the tight financial control to guide the company toward success—and the business suffers. Other companies do the opposite; they rely on their accountant to do *all* the work, and end up spending much more than necessary.

Hiring an individual accountant on a freelance basis—particularly if needed only part-time—is much cheaper than paying for a firm's vast overhead.

Find a happy medium. Hire an accountant to help with budgets, forecasts and cash flow statements, and to set up an accurate, easy daily bookkeeping system. For long-range financial planning and tax counseling, choose an accountant or CPA with conviction in his expertise, not someone who readily agrees to your every decision.

Extend credit with confidence

Accessing a larger pool of potential buyers comes at a considerable price. Collection departments plagued by inefficiency can overwork and expand your staff, inflate operating costs and dilute profits from each credit sale. Ineffective enforcement policies clog your cash flow. Though your sales may be booming, payments may trickle in sparingly. You may be forced to hire ineffective collection agencies or expensive lawyers. Worse yet, you may have to write off bad debt.

So how can your credit system run more efficiently and effectively? The key is to establish a positive, steady rapport with your debtors *from day one*. A complete collection of effective forms can guide you smoothly through each level of correspondence.

To process new accounts, you must access and evaluate your customer's credit history. This involves requests for bank and trade references, employment and insurance verification, financial statements, and lien checks. Practical analytical tools can help you choose those creditworthy applicants.

Once you extend credit, you must closely monitor payments collected. Although assignments and guarantees legally bind you to your debtor, they still cannot guarantee payments. Initial reminders to delinquent accounts should be friendly and understanding. If problems occur, work closely with customers to negotiate a reasonable payment plan. If necessary, become more assertive, cautioning against

You may not
CAUTION threaten, abuse,
or harass the
debtor. The Fair Debt
Collection Practices Act is
very strict regarding the
rights of the consumer.

penalties such as higher interest faster billing cycles, loss of future credit and even legal action. A helpful tool in collecting from your debtors is E-Z Legal's *Collecting Unpaid Bills Made E-Z.*

Effective communication is not always negative. Elicit regular payments with sales incentives or credit renewal. Or extend secured credit—usually with better rates and terms. Protect against loss by using standard personal guarantees, security agreements, conditional sales agreements and pledge agreements. If you suddenly discover a debtor's financial troubles, assert your rights to stop goods in transit or reclaim goods already sent.

> **The earlier you act upon outstanding debts, the better chances are of recovery.**

If all else fails, turn the account over to a collection agency or attorney, or you may begin the legal debt-collection process by filing the common litigation forms yourself. Collection should begin within 90 days. Collection agencies typically charge between 15 and 50 percent of the debt, the larger percentage for smaller transactions.

Analysis is equally as important as correspondence. Logs, balance sheets and reports help you review your program's effectiveness and improve your decision-making standards. If you have too many problem creditors, it is time to tighten up your policies. If few customers take advantage of your credit program, consider offering more attractive incentives. Finding that effective balance can make a big impact on your company's bottom line.

Alternatives to extending credit

If frustrated business owners had it their way, they would do away with the headache of extending credit and make all transactions cash-only. In reality, a company may have no choice but to extend credit to customers or risk losing significant market share to competitors who do.

Is extending credit appropriate or necessary to attract customers? A convenient alternative is to accept major credit cards. Credit card accounts are set up through banks, who readily accept most publicly-visible retailers but may hesitate with home-operated businesses. American Express accounts are handled directly and are often flexible with smaller ventures. Banks charge a processing fee, typically three to six percent. If you handle a large volume of credit card transactions, consider purchasing an electronic machine that hooks into the phone lines for instant approval and processing. Credit cards save you collection problems and protect you from stolen or invalid cards as long as you follow the routine procedures.

Credit Cautions

If you plan to extend credit, be sure your policies and procedures comply with all the federal government acts including the Fair Credit Billing, Equal Credit Opportunity, Consumer Credit Protection, Fair Credit Reporting, and Fair Debt Collection Practices Acts. They basically require you to disclose all terms and conditions of a loan and prohibit discrimination based on non-financial conditions. If you have questions, contact the Federal Trade Commission, Washington, D.C., 20580. Before you hire an attorney, consult an accountant to determine the role credit should play in your business.

You can lessen risk by refusing third party and temporary (or nameless) checks.

The same risk of extending credit applies to accepting checks. Be sure to ask for ID to verify address, phone number and signature. A "no personal checks" policy, if feasible, may also cut down on bad debt. More businesses are relying on a check authorization service. Similar to the major credit card programs, these companies charge a fee to validate questionable checking accounts by phone and insure against bounced checks. Once they authorize the check, they are responsible for paying you its face value minus their fee—even if the check bounces.

Taxes

The Internal Revenue Service never rests. They've created an increasingly complex and ever-changing labyrinth of tax forms even for tiny mom-and-pop operations. Tax time is a lot less hectic when your books are accurate, organized and up-to-date year round. Completing IRS forms can be largely a matter of plugging in figures from your Profit & Loss Statement and income and expense ledgers. There are many computer programs available to assist you, such as E-Z Legal's *W-2 Maker*.

 It may pay to hire an accountant to make sure you not only comply with legal requirements, but also maximize your deductions.

If you are a sole proprietor with no employees, pay no excise tax and did not inherit the business you may be able to use your Social Security Number for tax purposes. All other cases require a Federal Employer Identification Number (FEIN).

Calendar year vs. fiscal year

You will note that the IRS Request for Employer Identification Number asks for your fiscal year. In some states even the Certificate of Incorporation requires the fiscal year to be given. Of course, it is easiest to choose the calendar year as your corporation's fiscal year. However, if that is impossible, a second choice would be July 1 to June 30. In that case, for your first year of incorporation, you would have to file two sets of income tax forms: For the first half of the year you would file as a sole proprietor

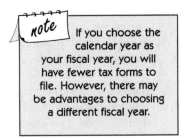 If you choose the calendar year as your fiscal year, you will have fewer tax forms to file. However, there may be advantages to choosing a different fiscal year.

(individual return) using Schedule C and any other appropriate schedules. For the second half of the year, you would file a corporate return (Form 1120, or Form 1120S if you make the Subchapter S election) and an individual return—because you are now an employee of your corporation.

Similarly, if you choose April 1 to October 1 as the beginning of your fiscal year, you will have to file the same two sets of tax returns. If you choose April 1, you would file as a sole proprietor for the first quarter (January 1 to March 31), and you would file corporate and individual returns for the last three quarters (April 1 to December 31). If you choose October 1 you would file as a sole proprietor for the first three quarters (January 1 to September 30), and you would file corporate and individual returns for the last quarter (October 1 to December 31).

 The advantage of a separate fiscal year is that it allows flexibility in tax planning. By having two tax years to work with, you and your accountant have more flexibility in tax planning. And the tax savings, corporate and personal, can be significant. You may want to choose a fiscal year on the advice of your accountant, who can determine the fiscal year most advantageous to you.

Tax information from the IRS

 Advice from an IRS agent is often unreliable. However, you can obtain surprisingly clear and helpful information from several IRS publications, including: Starting a Business and Keeping Records (IRS Publication 583), Tax Guide For Small Business (Pub. 334), Employer's Tax Guide (Circular E), Tax Calendars (Pub. 509), and Tax Withholding and Estimated Tax (Pub. 505). See the Resources section of this guide for IRS contact information.

Self-employment tax

Many people are not aware of the self-employment tax, also known as SECA (Self-Employment Contributions Act). According to 1997 figures, sole proprietorships, partners and active owners in LLCs must pay tax on business income if they earn more than $400 in a given year.

If you operate at a loss, you owe no income tax on the business. You can also apply this Net Operating Loss (NOL) to other taxable personal income or allow the credit to carry over to other years. If you are unable to generate profit over several years, the IRS may rule your venture is a "hobby" and disallow any tax benefits.

Employee and payroll taxes

If you hire employees, be prepared to devote about 30 percent of your payroll to taxes and paperwork. You are responsible for withholding all of your (full- or part-time) employees' federal and state income tax, Social Security and Medicare taxes from paychecks, remitting them with your overall tax bill. You also must pay your portion of Social Security and Medicare benefit funds. On employee salaries up to $65,400, you are taxed 6.2% for Social Security and 1.45% for Medicare (1997 figure).

Payroll taxes—including withholdings—are due quarterly on these dates:

- April 30 for wages paid January through March

- July 31 for April – June

- October 31 for July – September

- January 31 for October – December

If owed taxes exceed $500, the due date becomes the 15th day of the next month.

Independent contractors and taxes

You may be able to save paperwork and expenses by hiring independent contractors. These workers are in business for themselves, pay their own taxes and insurance, use their own equipment and facilities, require little or no supervision, and are typically paid per project. To avoid threat of tax fraud and liability charges, make sure the above factors apply, and make these points clear to the worker. A written Independent Contractors' Agreement is the best protection against potentially expensive or damaging misunderstandings.

When hiring an independent contractor, be sure to record his or her full name, address, and Social Security or Employer ID number.

Deducting business expenses

To qualify as a deduction from your taxable income, expenses must be business related, ordinary, necessary and reasonable. Keep accurate tabs on expenses by paying from your business account, entering expenses in the appropriate expense ledger category, and keeping all receipts. Expenses must be recorded as what you actually paid out—not market value. Interest charges for purchases are not deductible. Barter economy is treated like any other business income based on "fair market value."

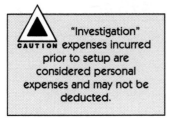

"Investigation" expenses incurred prior to setup are considered personal expenses and may not be deducted.

Deducting start-up costs can be complicated and may require the help of an accountant. Business-related start-up expenses may be deducted in one of two ways: capitalized at the time you quit or sell your business or amortized monthly over a 60-month period (see next section, Depreciation). The IRS also frequently denies deductions until the business actually makes a sale, although tax courts contend that as long as they operating they are "in business." In either case, it is a good idea to put off as many expenses as possible until you are "in business."

Depreciation

If you decide taxable profits at year's end are too small to warrant immediate deduction, you may choose to write the costs according to depreciation of any or all items with a life of over one year. This means you deduct the cost of an item divided over several years. Length of depreciation ranges from three to 39 years depending on the type of goods.

The cost of land on which a building is located cannot be depreciated.

Items you acquired before starting your operation may be depreciated based on their market value at the time you began using them for business. Major repairs and improvements may also be depreciated.

Personnel

10

Chapter 10

Personnel

What you'll find in this chapter:

➠ Why you are your best employee

➠ Learning when to delegate

➠ Acts that you should know about

➠ The workforce challenge

➠ Getting the most out of your employees

Managing employees effectively is critical to the performance of any company. To survive, you need to peacefully co-exist with your workers while complying with current laws and regulations. To thrive, you need to get the most out of your staff and mold them into a cohesive, productive unit. Whatever type of business you have, *your employees are your most valuable assets*; the sooner you realize this, the better off you'll be.

You are your best asset

As important as employees may be, the owner is the Most Valuable Player. You design the plays, and you call the shots. Anyone interested in your business plan will ask: "What do you bring to the table?" Document your experience, expertise, management capabilities and references by providing a thorough resume. Proof of financial responsibility is equally important.

Prepare a Personal Balance Sheet, obtain a copy of your credit reports and also include a record of your personal bank accounts and investments.

Sharing the workload

After dozens of endless, exhausting workweeks, you'll soon discover you can't do it all. The only way to gain control over your company—finding the time to make big decisions and to grow—is to effectively delegate authority and responsibility. To prosper, you must find able, trustworthy managers to help shoulder the load. Make sure your people know who is in charge of what and of whom; leave nothing to chance.

Avoid damaging legal conflicts

In these litigious times, misunderstandings and ambiguities in the workplace often lead to expensive lawsuits that can ruin your business. Most friction arises over verbal agreements, and even the sincerest intentions can be misconstrued. The best way to avoid trouble is to document everything in writing.

> ⚠ **CAUTION** An effective employee handbook clearly states rules and policies but must avoid unnecessary promises or guarantees.

A book of model forms and policies can serve as a valuable guide for your all written agreements. This can help you save time and keep everything standardized, from job applications to employment contracts, to listing benefits and disciplinary actions, to documenting termination procedures. Whether you need to hire a subcontractor or independent contractor, or enact an agreement pledging confidentiality, indemnity or non-competition, you can usually adapt the language of a standard form to meet your specific needs. E-Z Legal's *Managing Personnel Made E-Z* includes over 200 essential personnel forms covering everything from hiring to firing.

Know the laws that affect your business

The federal government has enacted volumes of laws to protect the rights of employers and employees. Complying with the rules that apply to your business is essential, so consult with your trade associations, business associates, insurance agent and attorney. An official may inspect your business, tell you what you need to change and when, or he may fine you. A few common laws are:

- ◆ *The Equal Employment Opportunity Act* governs discrimination issues in the workplace. It is illegal to base recruitment, testing, hiring, pay, benefits, promotion and firing of the workforce based upon race, religion, gender, age, veteran status or disability or other factors not related to legitimate job qualifications. Some state laws also include marital status and sexual orientation.

Appoint someone in your company to be responsible for compliance, and educate your employees about safety and other rules.

- ◆ *The Immigration and Naturalization Services (INS) Reform & Control Act* makes it crime to "knowingly hire an alien not authorized to work in the U.S." All applicants must show proof of U.S. citizenship or authorization to work in the U.S. before being hired. You must fill out the Employment Eligibility Verification Form I-9 (available from the local Immigration and Naturalization Service office) that requires you to check for at least one the following valid documents:

  - birth or naturalization certificate

  - U.S. passport

- foreign passport authorizing the person to work in the U.S. (e.g., a work visa)

- a green card authorizing work in the U.S.

- or a Social Security card and valid driver's license.

Applicants must also show proof of identification with one of the following:

- passport, driver's license, Certificate of U.S. Naturalization or Citizenship

- school photo ID

- draft card, military ID card, US Coast Guard ID card or military dependent's card

- voter registration card

- Native American tribal forms

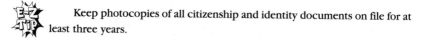 Keep photocopies of all citizenship and identity documents on file for at least three years.

♦ *The Fair Labor Standards Act* includes the *New Minimum Wage Act*. As of September 1, 1997, federal government raised the minimum wage to $5.15. Every business must post the new law even if you do not employ a single minimum wage worker or if you have only one employee. The act also requires an overtime rate of at least 1 1/2 times the regular pay rate for hourly employees, plus equal pay for women and child labor laws.

♦ *The Occupational Safety and Health Protection Act (OSHA)* features some 22,000 regulations governing workplace safety. The OSHA Institute near Chicago offers free training in all areas, including a comprehensive one-week program.

♦ *The Employee Retirement Income Security Act (ERISA)*, Consumer Products Safety Commission, Social Security Administration, and Labor Department also institute extensive legislation regarding the workplace.

It is your obligation to keep employees informed of their legal rights. Authorities can impose fines of up to $17,000 for businesses failing to post these acts at each work location:

- The Equal Employment Opportunity Act

- The Family Medical Leave Act

- The Employee Polygraph Protection Act

- The Fair Labor Standards Act

- The Occupational Safety and Health Protection Act must be posted by businesses with at least 50 employees. This number may soon change to 25.

The Federal Labor Law Poster available from E-Z Legal Forms contains these five laws to ensure your compliance.

The workforce challenge

Finding and keeping productive employees is a constant challenge for small businesses, particularly start-ups. Lower salaries, fewer benefits and less opportunity for advancement may not be enough to attract candidates beyond entry level. If you *are* able to land talented, ambitious workers, they typically use on-the-job training to advance to the next company. Studies show small businesses will lose 15 to 20 percent of its work force each year to larger companies; you could spend more time than expected placing ads, sifting through resumes and conducting interviews.

Make the most of your hiring process. Be aware of applicants who exaggerate job responsibilities, salaries, employment dates, educational merits and licensure. Calling to verify information is time-consuming but often necessary. A worthwhile interview involves more than a surface personality profile. Create ways to test an applicant's ability to perform practical job functions. And when you do hire an applicant, never make promises you can't keep or you may face a lawsuit.

Low-cost training

You may be able to obtain free or low-cost training through government agencies. Find out about the many seminars and training sessions offered by the Small Business Association. The Defense Department offers assistance in training and hiring those about to be released from the armed services. The government also offers grants and subsidies for vocational training of physically or emotionally handicapped workers.

Scale the motivational mountain

Any experienced manager will tell you: Workers are not machines. After you hire qualified employees, you need to motivate them to remain productive. Regardless of ability, each is driven by feelings of responsibility, accomplishment and appreciation. A boss who actively understands employees on both personal and professionals level is often more effective than one who keeps his distance but signs bigger checks. It is essential to encourage open lines of communication throughout your organization. This starts by establishing a clear, consistent set of policies that treat all employees equally and with respect—all the time.

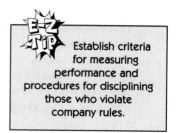

Establish criteria for measuring performance and procedures for disciplining those who violate company rules.

Here are a few more suggestions:

- Interact with new employees to discover their strengths and weaknesses.

- Offer challenges that put their specific abilities to maximum use.

- Try to minimize political friction by clearly establishing responsibilities and levels of authority.

- Evaluate performance on a regular basis.

- Keep morale high by encouraging workers to suggest improvements and air grievances.

- Tie incentives to performance to boost productivity.

Getting the help you need

Chapter 11

Getting the help you need

Information is power, and plenty of information is out there for the taking—available from competitors, field experts, government organizations and self-help publications. Don't rely solely on your own knowledge, as extensive as it may be. And don't ever be too proud to ask for advice or seek assistance from the resources around you. It could make the difference between failure and success for your business.

Study your competitors

Publicly held competitors represent a gold mine of market information. Annual 10-K reports, filed with the Security and Exchange Commission as a matter of public record, contain everything you need to know. Write to the company's director of investor relations to request this information or access 10-Ks through the Internet.

Privately held direct competitors, for obvious reasons, typically keep such inside information confidential. Still, you should be able to gain plenty of facts about your five nearest competitors by simply observing their day-to-day activities. You may also get information on smaller non-traded competitors from Dun & Bradstreet, a reputable database of company histories and credit profiles. In your Business Plan, be sure to list competitors' names and addresses, and analyze their product lines, prices and policies. Cite what you would do differently to give you the competitive edge.

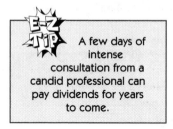

A few days of intense consultation from a candid professional can pay dividends for years to come.

No successful entrepreneur exists in a vacuum. Why not take the pulse of your indirect competition as well? Call businesses operating outside your area or offering products or services slightly different than yours. You may develop several contacts willing to share detailed stories about their successes and, even more importantly, their failures. Leaders in your field may be flattered to share time and ideas that will help you succeed.

Learning from those around you

Who knows your business better than your suppliers? They own first-hand knowledge of what sells, and they'll prove it to you with volumes of sales reports. With a vested interest, they will be eager to help you plan for your success, providing helpful input about everything from inventory and pricing to layout and promotion. They may also help you set up an inventory

Salespeople are always willing to share insights, from spotting trends and discovering hot sellers to constructing an effective merchandising mix and connecting people within the industry.

control system or even train your staff. Your bank may share a wealth of financial data on your customers and competition to help strengthen your business plan. But they expect initiative on your part, so show them you did your homework as well.

Trade associations serving your industry can be another valuable resource. They may be able to answer specific questions, or even provide published reports on aggregate statistics of similar businesses. Consult the Encyclopedia of Associations found in most libraries for addresses and phone numbers.

The Small Business Administration

The U.S. government wants your business to contribute to the gross national product. Uncle Sam provides a wide range of resources to get you started and help you grow, and the best resource for business start-ups is the Small Business Administration (SBA). See the Resources section of this guide for SBA information.

The SBA is known for guaranteeing loans to businesses turned down by other lenders. But the SBA offers much more than financing. It provides technical assistance to more than a million small businesses a year at over 900 Small Business

The SBA will help you locate professional loan packagers who tailor a business plan specifically for an SBA loan.

Development Centers across the country. Here you can take advantage of free or low-cost research assistance, consultation and training seminars for management and employees.

A key branch of the SBA is the Service Corps of Retired Executives (SCORE), over 13,000 veteran entrepreneurs who put their years of wisdom to work for you as free consultants. The SBA also pools the services of business professors, MBA students and undergrads at over 300 universities to help small businesses plan their start-ups. But bureaucratic delays often make the Small Business Institute Program an impractical option. You may decide to simply propose your business idea directly to a local college or university business professor. A class of young business students may eagerly research your potential customers, develop a marketing strategy and project your financial future. It provides them a lively opportunity to put textbook theories into practice. It provides you a thorough, albeit not expert, source of free information.

The Office of Advocacy

The Office of Advocacy is a division of the SBA whose mission is to encourage policies that support the development and growth of small business. They use economic research, regulatory advocacy and information resources to help small businesses.

Here are a few questions the Office of Advocacy can answer for a start-up business:

What is the definition of a small business?

DEFINITION For the purposes of the research performed by the Office of Advocacy, a *small business* is defined as an independently owned and operated firm with fewer than 500 employees. This size is often used as a short-hand definition of small business for other purposes but there is no statutory basis for it.

How many businesses are there?

As of 1995, there were approximately 22.5 million non-farm businesses, of which 99 percent are small by the size standards set by the U.S. Small Business Administration.

Where can I find statistics and research about my industry?

There are many sources for information on small businesses. The Office of Advocacy offers a catalog of research studies. Advocacy also provides statistics from U.S. Bureau of the Census and other sources, and a listing of recent research performed by the Office of Advocacy.

Is there anyone that I can contact about regulations and their impact?

First, the Office of Advocacy encourages small businesses to actively participate in the regulatory process by submitting comments to federal agencies about their policies and procedures. In addition, small businesses may contact the SBA about regulations.

> *note* The Office of Advocacy also is interested in regulatory or research initiatives that would benefit small businesses.

One part of the Office of Advocacy's mission is to monitor federal agencies' efforts to minimize the impact of regulations on small businesses. As required by the Regulatory Flexibility Act, Advocacy regularly reviews and comments on agencies' proposed rules and regulatory analyses. Small businesses concerned about regulations under development by federal agencies should contact Advocacy.

For questions about regulatory compliance, small businesses should contact federal agencies. For information about agencies' resources, visit the U.S. Business Advisor. As a result of the Small Business Regulatory Enforcement Fairness Act, federal agencies must have a inquiry process in place by March 1997, to respond to small businesses' question about compliance. Small businesses that encounter problems with the enforcement aspects of regulations, may contact the SBA's Small Business and Agriculture Enforcement Ombudsman. (The Ombudsman is not part of the Office of Advocacy.) The Ombudsman position was established by the Small Business Regulatory Enforcement Fairness Act of 1996.

Other government resources

The *U.S. Census Bureau* can supply you with a raw demographic breakdown of your area. The Treasury and Commerce departments have a mountain of statistics on sales, market concentration and the number of firms in any given industry. Metropolitan libraries have also gathered all the resources you need.

Thinking of developing a new product? Write the *U.S. Patent Office* and they will send you a list of inventions you can buy or license. If you have a specific technical problem, a team of researchers awaits your letter at the Science and Technology Division of the Congressional Library in the nation's capitol. They will send you a detailed report on the subject within weeks.

The U.S. Government is the country's largest single purchaser of goods and services. Learn about Uncle Sam's needs through the Provisions Governing Qualifications, published in many trade magazines or available from the *U.S. Department of Commerce*. You can also read that department's publication, Commerce Business Daily, or subscribe to the SBA's Bidder's Early Message (BEAM) by contacting the SBA. If your products and/or services are tested and meet the government agency's performance or design standards, they will make the Qualified Products List. This enables you to bid on often-lucrative government contracts.

Have you thought of entering the international market? If so, you can get plenty of help from several government agencies including the Import-Export Bank and the *Commerce Department Bureau of International Commerce*. The SBA also hosts U.S. Export Assistance Centers in 15 cities.

Other helpful departments include:

• *The Consumer Information Center (CIC)*, which offers a consumer information catalog of federal publications.

• *The Consumer Product Safety Commission (CPSC)*, which offers guidelines for product safety requirements.

• *The U.S. Department of Agriculture (USDA)*, which offers publications on selling to the USDA. Publications and programs on entrepreneurship are also available through county extension offices nationwide.

• *The U.S. Department of Commerce (DOC)*, whose Business Assistance Center provides listings of business opportunities available in the federal government. This service also will refer businesses to different programs and services in the DOC and other federal agencies.

• *The U.S. Department of Labor (DOL)*, which offers publications on compliance with labor laws.

• *The U.S. Department of Treasury* and its *Internal Revenue Service (IRS)* which offer information on tax requirements for small businesses.

• *The U.S. Environmental Protection Agency (EPA)*, which offers more than 100 publications designed to help small businesses understand how they can comply with EPA regulations.

• *The U.S. Food and Drug Administration (FDA)*, which offers information on packaging and labeling requirements for food and food-related products.

Other sources of information

A librarian can help you locate the specific information you need in reference books. Most libraries have a variety of directories, indexes and encyclopedias that cover many business topics. They also have other resources, such as:

Trade association information

Ask the librarian to show you a directory of trade associations. Associations provide a valuable network of resources to their members through publications and services such as newsletters, conferences and seminars.

Books

Many guidebooks, textbooks and manuals on small business are published annually. To find the names of books not in your local library check Books In Prints, a directory of books currently available from publishers.

Magazine and newspaper articles

Business and professional magazines provide information that is more current than that found in books and textbooks. There are a number of indexes to help you find specific articles in periodicals.

 In addition to books and magazines, many libraries offer free workshops, lend skill-building tapes and have catalogues and brochures describing continuing education opportunities.

The Internet

If you have a computer and access to the World Wide Web, then you have a wealth of information at your fingertips. The Resources section of the guide lists dozens of sites that contain useful information to help any fledgling business get started.

Small business facts

Chapter 12
Small business facts

Business dissolution

Of every seven businesses which shut their doors, only one of seven actually fails—that is, leaves unpaid obligations (Source: SBA-sponsored research). Business failures and bankruptcies both declined during 1995. Failures declined 0.5 percent, to 71,194 from 71,558. Business bankruptcies also declined 0.5 percent, from 50,845 in 1994 to 50,516 in 1995. (Source: Dun and Bradstreet; Administrative Office of the U.S. Courts)

Women- and minority-owned firms

According to a 1995 study by the National Foundation for Women Business Owners and Dun and Bradstreet (a company that gathers data on businesses), there are now 7.7 million women-owned firms providing jobs for 15.5 million persons, more than that employed by Fortune 500 industrial firms.

Data on women- and black-owned businesses for 1987 and 1992 reveal that these businesses fared well in the strong economy of the late 1980s. Between 1987 and 1992 the number of women-owned businesses rose from 4,112,787 to 5,888,883, an increase of about 43 percent. The total receipts of women-owned businesses nearly tripled over this same time period, rising from $278.1 billion in 1987 to $642.5 billion in 1992. The Census Bureau also reported 517,000 women-owned large corporations in 1992. Including large, women-owned corporations, there were 6.4 million women-owned firms, with receipts of $1.6 billion in 1992. These firms represented 32 percent of all firms in 1992.

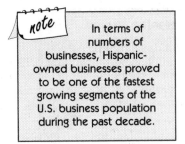

note

In terms of numbers of businesses, Hispanic-owned businesses proved to be one of the fastest growing segments of the U.S. business population during the past decade.

During the 1987-1992 period, the number of black-owned businesses rose by 46 percent, from 424,165 to 620,912. As of 1992, the receipts of black-owned businesses totaled $32.2 billion, almost double their $19.8 billion in receipts in 1987. Between 1987 and 1992, the latest years available, the number of Hispanic-owned businesses rose from 422,373 to 771,708, an increase of 82.7 percent; their total receipts rose from $24.7 billion in 1987 to $72.8 billion in 1992.

Businesses owned by Asian Americans, American Indians, and other minorities increased by 87.2 percent between 1982 and 1987. This was the fastest increase of all the minority business groups surveyed by the Bureau of the Census for those years.

In addition, with the exception of non-minority male-owned firms, firms owned by Asian Americans, American Indians, and other minorities had the highest average receipts in 1987, $90,350 per firm. By contrast, all firms in the economy within the scope of Census surveys had average receipts of $145,654 in 1987, while Black and Hispanic firms averaged $46,593 and $58,554 in receipts, respectively. (All of the 1992 Census data on minority-owned firms should be available before the end of 1996.)

Procurement

In fiscal year (FY) 1994, the federal government spent $196.4 billion for the acquisition of supplies and equipment, construction services, research and development, and a variety of other services. Awards to small firms accounted for 31 percent of this total, or $61.7 billion. This includes $39.7 billion (20.2 percent) in awards made directly to small firms working for the federal government and $22.0 billion (11.2 percent) in subcontracting awards which small businesses received from prime contractors working under contract to the federal government. Of the $39.7 billion awarded directly to small firms, over $28.4 billion were in contract actions over $25,000, and $11.3 billion were in contract actions under $25,000.

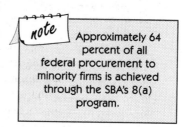

note Approximately 64 percent of all federal procurement to minority firms is achieved through the SBA's 8(a) program.

In FY 1994, approximately $5.2 billion was awarded to minority-owned firms through the 8(a) program. Minority-owned firms received approximately 5.2 percent of all federal procurement in FY 1994, while women-owned firms received 1.3 percent. (Source: Federal Procurement Data Center; Department of Defense)

Income

The income of non-farm proprietors and partners rose to $449.2 billion during 1995, up from $415.9 billion during 1994, an increase of 8.0 percent. By contrast, the compensation of employees rose 5.0 percent during 1995. (Source: U.S. Department of Commerce, Bureau of Economic Analysis)

While non-farm proprietors' income is only about 10 percent of total employee compensation (wages and salaries), about 85 percent of small firms are organized as proprietorships or partnerships. Therefore, for a majority of small business owners, 1995 was an especially good year in regard to income.

Employment

Between December 1994 and December 1995, employment in small business-dominated industries increased 2.7 percent, generating 1.25 million new jobs, or 75 percent of the total (Source: Office of Advocacy research). Small microbusinesses with 1 to 4 employees generated about 35 percent of the net new jobs, while firms with 5 to 19 employees created another 32 percent of new employment opportunities.

During the 1991-1995 period, there were about 7.7 million net new jobs added to the economy. Since 1993, almost 10 million new jobs have been created across the entire economy. The fastest growing sectors of small business-dominated industries during the past several years include restaurants, outpatient care facilities, office of physicians, special trade construction contractors, computer and data processing services, credit reporting and collection firms, medical and dental laboratories, providers of day care, and counseling and rehabilitation services. (Source: U.S. Department of Labor; Office of Advocacy research)

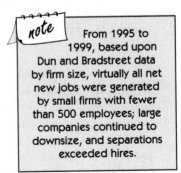

note From 1995 to 1999, based upon Dun and Bradstreet data by firm size, virtually all net new jobs were generated by small firms with fewer than 500 employees; large companies continued to downsize, and separations exceeded hires.

According to recent projections issued by the Bureau of Labor Statistics, small firm-dominated sectors of the economy will contribute about 60 percent of new jobs between 1994 and 2005. (Large firms will contribute 15 percent, and industries dominated by neither large nor small firms—such as business services—will contribute the remainder.) About 88 percent of these jobs will be in retail trade or services.

Some of the fastest growing small business-dominated sectors during this period will be medical and dental laboratories, up 84 percent; residential care industries (related to housing of the elderly, group homes, and social services such as drug rehabilitation), up 83 percent; credit reporting, up 68 percent; equipment leasing, up 51 percent; child day care services, up 59 percent; and job training, up 43 percent. Jobs in some of the highest paying service sectors—such as in offices of physicians, and architectural and engineering services—will rise about 30 percent, In addition, the restaurant industry (always a prolific small business job creator) is projected to add 1.02 million new jobs between 1994 and 2005.

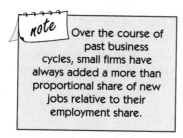

note Over the course of past business cycles, small firms have always added a more than proportional share of new jobs relative to their employment share.

During the entire 1976-1990 period, small firms (that is, those with less than 500 employees) provided 53 percent of total employment and 65 percent of net new jobs. (Source: SBA-sponsored research, Dun and Bradstreet data) From 1991 to 1993, according to the latest Census data (produced under contract for SBA), small firms with 0 to 4 employees created most of the net new jobs. Of the gross jobs created, 821,000 came from expansions of new small firms with 0 to 4 employees which moved into the 5 to 19 employee firm-size category. Some 701,000 jobs came from firms with 5 to 19 employees that grew to have 20 to 49 employees. A major share of jobs also came from births of new small firms.

The small business share of net new jobs increases most rapidly during the recovery stage of a cycle, and during the earlier parts of the expansion phase of a cycle. As the economy approaches full employment during the latter stages of an expansion, larger firms tend to produce a larger share of jobs, while the small business share falls somewhat. (Source: The State of Small Business, A Report of the President, printed by the U.S.G.P.O.)

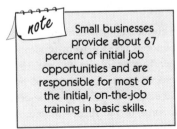

Small businesses provide about 67 percent of initial job opportunities and are responsible for most of the initial, on-the-job training in basic skills.

Jobs generated by small firms are more likely to be filled by younger workers, older workers, and women. Many of these workers prefer, or are only able, to work on a part-time basis, and thus can be easily accommodated by small employers. (Source: The State of Small Business, A Report of the President, printed by the U.S.G.P.O.)

High-technology employment

Small firms (those with less than 500 employees) provided 35 percent of the jobs in high-technology industries. These 73,550 small high-technology companies had receipts of $160.9 billion, or 25 percent of the industry total. About 93 percent of high-technology firms have less than 500 employees; 70 percent have less than 20 employees.

Financing

Overall, small firms rely more on owner capital and less on external debt capital compared to larger firms. Small firms are also more dependent than large firms on short-term debt. Most small firms use external financing only occasionally. Less than 50 percent of small firms borrow once or more during a year. However, a portion of small firms—those experiencing rapid growth or those with high volumes of receivable—require frequent use of external financing.

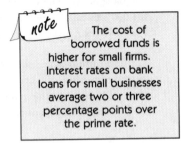

The cost of borrowed funds is higher for small firms. Interest rates on bank loans for small businesses average two or three percentage points over the prime rate.

The majority of small firms used some form of financing in the past. The recently completed National Survey of Small Firm Financing (co-funded by the SBA and the Federal Reserve), which examined firms with 1 to 499 employees, revealed the following financing patterns.

Credit cards are also a very important financing source. 39 percent of small businesses use personal credit cards for business purposes and 28 percent use business credit cards. Use of a personal credit card is more common for very small firms: about 40 percent of firms with fewer than 10 employees use personal credit cards, compared to 23 percent of larger firms (those with 50 or more employees).

Of larger small businesses (those with 100 to 499 employees), 60 percent have lines of credit, 30 percent have financial leases, 19 percent have mortgage loans, 29 percent have equipment loans, and 26 percent have motor vehicle loans. Thirty-seven percent of small firms obtained some form of financing from commercial banks. Other major suppliers include finance companies, leasing companies, and other non-financial institutions. Total business loans outstanding to small firms by commercial banks (as approximated by loan size of under $250,000) amount to $164 billion, accounting for 20.3 percent of total business lending by banks.

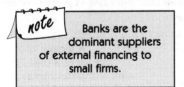

note

Banks are the dominant suppliers of external financing to small firms.

For the smallest firms—that is, those "mom-and-pop" operations with or without hired employees—owner capital is the most important source of financing. Other sources of financing include trade credit, personal loans from financial institutions, and loans from friends and relatives.

Innovation

Small firms produce 55 percent of innovations. Small firms produce twice as many product innovations per employee as large firms, including the employees of firms that do not innovate. This is also true of significant innovations. Small firms obtain more patents per sales dollar, even though large firms are more likely to patent a discovery, implying that small firms have more discoveries. Small research and development (R&D) firms are quite research intensive; the percentage of employees that are R&D scientists and engineers are 6.41 percent in small firms and 4.05 percent in large R&D firms.

Large firms receive 26 percent of their research and development dollars from the federal government and are more dependent on federal R&D dollars than small firms, which receive only 11 percent of their R&D funds from the federal government. The rate of return on R&D expenditures is 26 percent for both small and large firms, but only 14 percent for firms not involved with a university. The estimated rates of return on total R&D for firms with a university relationship are 30 percent for large firms and 44 percent for small firms. The average small enterprise with intellectual property has 61 employees with 19 percent of the employees in R&D, and the average large enterprise with intellectual property has 12,879 employees with 3 percent of the employees in R&D.

note A federal R&D dollar to a small firm is more than four times as likely to be used for basic research as a federal R&D dollar to a large firm.

Innovations coming from small high-tech firms are expected to increase in the coming years as a result of the increase in the federal Small Business Innovation Research (SBIR) program. Under this program, federal agencies with large research and development budgets must direct designated amounts of their R&D contracts to small firms—the source of 55 percent of innovations and new technologies.

Since the inception of the SBIR program in fiscal year 1983, almost $4 billion in competitive federal R&D awards have been made to qualified small business concerns under the program. Among the important innovations by U.S. small firms in the 20th century are the airplane, audio tape recorder, double-knit fabric, fiber optic examining equipment, heart valve, optical scanner, pacemaker, personal computer, soft contact lenses, and the zipper.

The forms in this guide

Accounting

Credit

Personnel

BUSINESS PLAN

FOR

_____

BUSINESS PLAN:
CONTENTS

PART I: IDENTIFYING INFORMATION

PART II: STATEMENT OF PURPOSE

PART III: MANAGEMENT

PART IV: MARKETING

PART V: PRODUCTION

PART VI: FINANCES

PART VII: OTHER INFORMATION

ADDENDUM (Documents Attached):

   Financial Data
   Tax Documents
   Contracts
   Leases and Licenses
   Corporate Bylaws or Partnership/LLC agreement
   Additional Documents

BUSINESS PLAN, PART I
IDENTIFYING INFORMATION

Name of Company: _____

DBA Name(s): _____

Address: _____

_____

Telephone(s): _____

Fax: _____   E-mail: _____

Description of Business: _____

_____

_____

Form of Business Entity: _____ Date Formed: _____

For a New Business:
The nature and purpose of the business shall be: _____

_____

_____

_____

For an Existing Business:
Length of Operation: _____

The nature of the expansion of the business is: _____

_____

_____

_____

BUSINESS PLAN, PART II
STATEMENT OF PURPOSE

The nature and purpose of this company is: _____

_____

_____

_____

_____

The history of this company's development is: _____

_____

_____

_____

The nature of the product and/or service shall be: _____

_____

_____

_____

The manner in which this product/service shall be created is: _____

_____

_____

_____

_____

BUSINESS PLAN, PART III
MANAGEMENT

The members/directors/partners/managers of the business are:

Name _____

Address _____

_____

Phone/Fax _____

E-mail _____

Position _____

Contributions to Business Shall Be: _____

_____

Name _____

Address _____

_____

Phone/Fax _____

E-mail _____

Position _____

Contributions to Business Shall Be: _____

_____

Name _____

Address _____

_____

Phone/Fax _____

E-mail _____

Position _____

Contributions to Business Shall Be: _____

_____

Name _____

Address _____

_____

Phone/Fax _____

E-mail _____

Position _____

Contributions to Business Shall Be: _____

_____

Name _____

Address _____

_____

Phone/Fax _____

E-mail _____

Position _____

Contributions to Business Shall Be: _____

_____

Name _____

Address _____

_____

Phone/Fax _____

E-mail _____

Position _____

Contributions to Business Shall Be: _____

_____

Professional, technical and other support to be received by the business:

Name _____   Name _____

Address _____   Address _____

_____   _____

Phone/Fax _____   Phone/Fax _____

E-mail _____   E-mail_____

Service to be Performed _____   Service to be Performed _____

_____   _____

Compensation Paid _____   Compensation Paid _____

Name _____   Name _____

Address _____   Address _____

_____   _____

Phone/Fax _____   Phone/Fax _____

E-mail _____   E-mail_____

Service to be Performed _____   Service to be Performed _____

_____   _____

Compensation Paid _____   Compensation Paid _____

The management structure of the business shall be: _____

_____

_____

_____

_____

BUSINESS PLAN, PART IV
MARKETING

Market Area: _____

_____

Market Potential: _____

_____

Consumer Customers: _____

_____

Commercial Customers: _____

_____

Competition: _____

_____

Advantage over competitors: _____

_____

Sales forecast by category: _____

_____

_____

Sales and distribution plan: _____

_____

_____

141

BUSINESS PLAN, PART V
PRODUCTION

Description of Facilities: _____

_____

_____

Description of Equipment: _____

_____

_____

Labor requirements: _____

_____

Supplies requirements: _____

_____

Shipping/transportation: _____

_____

Quality control: _____

_____

Special workforce plans/programs: _____

_____

_____

142

Outline of daily operations:

_____

_____

_____

_____

_____

_____

_____

BUSINESS PLAN, PART VI
FINANCES

Projected Income by Quarter:

_____	_____	_____	_____
1st quarter	2nd quarter	3rd quarter	4th quarter

Relevant Information:_____

_____

_____

_____

Projected Expenses by Quarter:

_____	_____	_____	_____
1st quarter	2nd quarter	3rd quarter	4th quarter

Relevant Information:_____

_____

_____

_____

Projected Assets/Liabilities:

        Current Assets: _____

        Fixed Assets: _____

        Other Assets: _____

        Current Liabilities: _____

        Long-term Liabilities: _____

        Net Worth: _____

Financial Goals:

Annual Sales $ _____   Current Ratio _____   to _____

Annual Profits $ _____   Debt-Net Worth Ratio _____   to _____

Bondability $ _____

BUSINESS PLAN, PART VII
OTHER INFORMATION

INSURANCE

Company _____ Policy # _____

Coverage _____ Premium _____

LOANS/OUTSTANDING DEBTS

Lender _____

Original Amount _____ Balance Unpaid _____

COMPETITIVE PROJECTIONS

Other resources needed to become competitive: _____

_____

_____

Years projected to become competitive: _____

LICENSES/PERMITS/CERTIFICATES

Type	Amount	Issuer
_____	_____	_____
_____	_____	_____
_____	_____	_____
_____	_____	_____
_____	_____	_____

MISCELLANEOUS

Trade Associations/Organizations of Membership: _____

_____

_____

_____

_____

Contracts With Suppliers: _____

_____

_____

_____

Liens, Judgments, or Lawsuits in Force or Pending: _____

_____

_____

Patents, Royalties, Copyrights, etc.:_____

_____

_____

_____

_____

MARKETING PLAN

This is the marketing plan of _____

I. MARKET ANALYSIS
    A. Target Market - Who are the customers?
        1. We will be selling primarily to (check all that apply):

		Total Percent of Business
a. Private sector	_____	_____
b. Wholesalers	_____	_____
c. Retailers	_____	_____
d. Government	_____	_____
e. Other	_____	_____

        2. We will be targeting customers by:

            a. Product line/services.
               We will target specific lines   _____
            b. Geographic area? Which areas? _____
            c. Sales? We will target sales of _____
            d. Industry? Our target industry is _____
            e. Other? _____

        3. How much will our selected market spend on our type of product or service this coming year?

                              $ _____

    B. Competition
        1. Who are our competitors?

            NAME   _____
            ADDRESS   _____
                       _____

            Years in Business   _____
            Market Share   _____
            Price/Strategy   _____
            Product/Service Features _____

NAME

ADDRESS _____

_____

Years in Business   _____

Market Share   _____

Price/Strategy   _____

Product/Service Features _____

2. How competitive is the market?

High   _____

Medium   _____

Low   _____

3. List below your strengths and weaknesses compared to your competition (consider such areas as location, size of resources, reputation, services, personnel, etc.):

Strengths	Weaknesses
1. _____	1. _____
2. _____	2. _____
3. _____	3. _____
4. _____	4. _____

C. Environment

1. The following are some important economic factors that will affect our product or service (such as trade area growth, industry health, economic trends, taxes, rising energy prices, etc.):

_____

_____

_____

2. The following are some important legal factors that will affect our market:

_____

_____

_____

3. The following are some important government factors:

_____

_____

_____

4. The following are other environmental factors that will affect our market, but over which we have no control:

_____

_____

_____

_____

II. PRODUCT OR SERVICE ANALYSIS
A. Description
1. Describe here what the product/service is and what it does:

_____

_____

_____

_____

B. Comparison
1. What advantages does our product/service have over those of the competition (consider such things as unique features, patents, expertise, special training, etc.)?

_____

_____

_____

_____

2. What disadvantages does it have?

_____

_____

_____

_____

C. Some Considerations
1. Where will you get your materials and supplies?

_____

_____

2. List other considerations:

_____

_____

_____

_____

III. MARKETING STRATEGIES - MARKET MIX

A. Image
What kind of image do we want to have (such as cheap but good, or exclusiveness, or customer-oriented or highest quality, or convenience, or speed, or ...)?

_____

B. Features
List the features we will emphasize:

    a. _____

    b. _____

    c. _____

C. Pricing
1. We will be using the following pricing strategy:

    a. Markup on cost   _____   What % markup?   _____

    b. Suggested price   _____

    c. Competitive   _____

    d. Below competition _____

    e. Premium price   _____

    f. Other   _____

2. Are our prices in line with our image?
YES_____ NO_____
3. Do our prices cover costs and leave a margin of profit?
YES_____ NO_____

D. Customer Services
1. List the customer services we provide:

    a. _____

    b. _____

    c. _____

2. These are our sales/credit terms:

    a. _____

    b. _____

    c. _____

3. The competition offers the following services:

    a. _____

    b. _____

    c. _____

E. Advertising/Promotion
   1. These are the things we wish to say about the business:

   _____

   _____

   _____

   2. We will use the following advertising/promotion sources:
      1. Television   _____
      2. Radio   _____
      3. Direct mail   _____
      4. Personal contacts   _____
      5. Trade associations   _____
      6. Newspaper   _____
      7. Magazines   _____
      8. Yellow Pages   _____
      9. Billboard   _____
      10. Other_____   _____

   3. The following are the reasons why we consider the media we have chosen to be the
      most effective:

   _____

   _____

   _____

APPLICATION FOR REGISTRATION
OF FICTITIOUS/ASSUMED NAME
(FOR CORPORATION/PARTNERSHIP DOING BUSINESS UNDER ASSUMED NAME)

I HEREBY CERTIFY that I am conducting or transacting business under the assumed

name of

at   City or Town of   ,

County of   , State of   .

The corporation's name is:

and the principal place of business is:

I FURTHER CERTIFY that I am the successor in interest to

the person or persons heretofore using such name or names to conduct or transact business.

IN WITNESS WHEREOF, I have this   day of   ,   (year),

executed this certificate.

_____

Business Operator

State of
County of
On   before me,   ,
appeared
personally known to me (or proved to me on the basis of satisfactory evidence) to be the person(s)
whose name(s) is/are subscribed to the within instrument and acknowledged to me that
he/she/they executed the same in his/her/their authorized capacity(ies), and that by his/her/their
signature(s) on the instrument the person(s), or the entity upon behalf of which the person(s)
acted, executed the instrument.

WITNESS my hand and official seal.

Signature_____   Affiant _____Known_____Produced ID
                                              Type of ID_____

(Seal)

152

APPLICATION FOR REGISTRATION
OF FICTITIOUS/ASSUMED NAME

(FOR INDIVIDUAL DOING BUSINESS UNDER ASSUMED NAME)

I HEREBY CERTIFY that I am conducting or transacting business under the assumed name of

at   City or Town of   ,

County of   , State of   .

My full legal name is:*

and my address is:

I FURTHER CERTIFY that I am the successor in interest to the person or persons heretofore using such name or names to conduct or transact business.

IN WITNESS WHEREOF, I have this   day of   ,   (year), executed this certificate.

_____

Business Operator

*If under 21 years of age, state "I am _____ years of age."

State of
County of
On   before me,   ,
appeared
personally known to me (or proved to me on the basis of satisfactory evidence) to be the person(s) whose name(s) is/are subscribed to the within instrument and acknowledged to me that he/she/they executed the same in his/her/their authorized capacity(ies), and that by his/her/their signature(s) on the instrument the person(s), or the entity upon behalf of which the person(s) acted, executed the instrument.
WITNESS my hand and official seal.

Signature_____   Affiant _____Known_____Produced ID
                                             Type of ID_____

(Seal)

N.Y. CERTIFICATE TO CONDUCT BUSINESS—INDIVIDUAL

CERTIFICATE UNDER SECTION 130 OF THE GENERAL BUSINESS LAW
RELATING TO CONDUCT OF BUSINESS UNDER THE NAME OF

_____

Pursuant to section 130 of the General Business Law, I hereby certify that:

1. I intend to transact or conduct business in the State of New York within the county of
under the name or designation of
       at

2. My full name is   , and I reside at

3. I am not less than eighteen years of age [I am less than eighteen years of age, to wit:
years of age].

_____   _____
Signature   Type Name

State of   )
County of   )
On   before me,   ,
personally appeared   , personally known to me (or
proved to me on the basis of satisfactory evidence) to be the person(s) whose name(s) is/are subscribed to the within instrument and acknowledged to me that he/she/they executed the same in
his/her/their authorized capacity(ies), and that by his/her/their signature(s) on the instrument the
person(s), or the entity upon behalf of which the person(s) acted, executed the instrument.
WITNESS my hand and official seal.

Signature_____   Affiant _____ Known   _____Produced ID
       Signature of Notary   Type of ID _____
                                                                  (Seal)

154

N.Y. CERTIFICATE TO CONDUCT BUSINESS—PARTNERSHIP

CERTIFICATE UNDER SECTION 130 OF THE GENERAL BUSINESS
LAW RELATING TO CONDUCT OF BUSINESS UNDER THE NAME OF

_____

Pursuant to section 130 of the General Business Law, the undersigned persons, who are carrying on, conducting, or transacting business in the State of New York as members of a partnership, do hereby certify that:

1. They intend to conduct or transact business as members of a partnership within the county of
    under the name or designation of
    at   .

2. They constitute all the members of the partnership hereinabove mentioned.

3. Their full names and residence addresses are:

Full Name   Residence Address

_____   _____

_____   _____

_____   _____

4. Each of them is at least eighteen years of age [, except for
    , who is   years of age].

_____   _____
Signature   Type Name

_____   _____
Signature   Type Name

_____   _____
Signature   Type Name

State of   )
County of   )
On   before me,   , personally appeared
                     , personally known to me (or proved to me on the basis of satisfactory evidence) to be the person(s) whose name(s) is/are subscribed to the within instrument and acknowledged to me that he/she/they executed the same in his/her/their authorized capacity(ies), and that by his/her/their signature(s) on the instrument the person(s), or the entity upon behalf of which the person(s) acted, executed the instrument.

WITNESS my hand and official seal.

Signature_____   Affiant _____ Known   _____Produced ID
         Signature of Notary   Type of ID _____
                                                                                   (Seal)

State of   )
County of   )
On   before me,   , personally appeared
                     , personally known to me (or proved to me on the basis of satisfactory evidence) to be the person(s) whose name(s) is/are subscribed to the within instrument and acknowledged to me that he/she/they executed the same in his/her/their authorized capacity(ies), and that by his/her/their signature(s) on the instrument the person(s), or the entity upon behalf of which the person(s) acted, executed the instrument.

WITNESS my hand and official seal.

Signature_____   Affiant _____ Known   _____Produced ID
         Signature of Notary   Type of ID _____
                                                                                   (Seal)

N.Y. CERTIFICATE TO CONDUCT BUSINESS—CORPORATION
CERTIFICATE RELATING TO CONDUCT OF BUSINESS
UNDER ASSUMED NAME BY CORPORATION

New York State
DEPARTMENT OF STATE
CORPORATIONS AND STATE RECORDS DIVISION
162 Washington Avenue
Albany, NY 12231

CORPORATION—CERTIFICATE OF ASSUMED NAME
(Pursuant to Section 130 General Business Law)

FEES: FOR THE FILING FEE PAYABLE TO THE SECRETARY OF STATE PLUS THE FEE FOR EACH COUNTY LISTED IN WHICH BUSINESS WILL BE TRANSACTED UNDER ASSUMED NAME, SEE GENERAL BUSINESS LAW s 130(5) AND CPLR s 8021(b)(2).

1. Corporation Name: _____

2. Law corporation formed under:
   ❑ Business   ❑ Not-for-Profit   ❑ Education   ❑ Insurance
   ❑ Other (specify) _____

3. Assumed Name: _____

4. Principal place of business in New York State:

   _____
   No. and Street

   _____
   City   State   Zip Code   County

   ❑ If none, check box and insert principal out-of-state address above.

5. Counties in which business will be conducted under assumed name (check one box):
   ❑ All counties   ❑ If not all, circle which counties below:

Albany	Columbia	Greene	Nassau	Onondaga	St. Lawrence	Tioga
Allegheny	Cortland	Hamilton	New York	Ontario	Saratoga	Tompkins
Broome	Delaware	Herkimer	City Bronx	Orange	Schenectady	Ulster
Cattaraugus	Dutchess	Jefferson	Kings	Orleans	Schoharie	Warren
Cayuga	Erie	Lewis	New York	Oswego	Schuyler	Washington
Chautauqua	Essex	Livingston	Queens	Otsego	Seneca	Wayne
Chemung	Franklin	Madison	Richmond	Putnam	Steuben	Westchester
Chenango	Fulton	Monroe	Niagara	Rensselaer	Suffolk	Wyoming
Clinton	Genesee	Montgomery	Oneida	Rockland	Sullivan	Yates

6. The addresses of each location within New York State where business is or will be conducted under assumed name—list on reverse side. If no business locations in New York State, check this box: ❑

156

Corporation Officer Signature:_____

Type Name and Office:_____

State of   )

County of   )

On   before me,   , personally appeared _____, personally known to me (or proved to me on the basis of satisfactory evidence) to be the person(s) whose name(s) is/are subscribed to the within instrument and the of   ,   the corporation described in the forgoing certificate, and acknowledged to me that he/she/they executed the same in his/her/their authorized capacity(ies) by order of the board of directors of such corporation, and that by his/her/their signature(s) on the instrument the person(s), or the entity upon behalf of which the person(s) acted, executed the instrument.

WITNESS my hand and official seal.

Signature_____   Affiant _____ Known   _____Produced ID
            Signature of Notary   Type of ID _____
                                                                (Seal)

Filer's Name _____ Date Filed _____

Filer's Address _____
            No. and Street   City   State   Zip Code

7. Addresses or business locations:

No. & Street		No. & Street	
City	State	City	State
Zip Code	County	Zip Code	County
No. & Street		No. & Street	
City	State	City	State
Zip Code	County	Zip Code	County
No. & Street		No. & Street	
City	State	City	State
Zip Code	County	Zip Code	County

USE CONTINUATION SHEET IF NECESSARY.

ASSIGNMENT OF ASSETS

TO

_____

BE IT KNOWN, for value received, the undersigned   of

hereby unconditionally and irrevocably assigns and trans-

fers unto   of   all right, title and

interest in and to the following:

The undersigned fully warrants that it has full rights and authority to enter into this assignment and that the rights and benefits assigned hereunder are free and clear of any lien, encumbrance, adverse claim or interest by any third party.

This assignment shall be binding upon and inure to the benefit of the parties, and their successors and assigns.

Signed this   day of   (year).

_____   _____
Witness' Signature   Assignor's Signature

_____   _____
Print Name of Witness   Print Name of Assignor

_____   _____
Address of Witness   Address of Assignor

_____   _____
Witness' Signature   Assignee's Signature

_____   _____
Print Name of Witness   Print Name of Assignee

_____   _____
Address of Witness   Address of Assignee

BILL OF SALE

FOR VALUE RECEIVED, the undersigned

of _____ hereby sells and transfers unto

_____ of _____ (Buyer),

and its successors and assigns forever, the following described goods and chattels:

Seller warrants and represents that it has good title to said property, full authority to sell and transfer same and that said goods and chattels are being sold free and clear of all liens, encumbrances, liabilities and adverse claims, of every nature and description.

Seller further warrants that it shall fully defend, protect, indemnify and save harmless the Buyer and its lawful successors and assigns from any and all adverse claim, that may be made by any party against said goods.

It is provided, however, that Seller disclaims any implied warranty of condition, merchantability or fitness for a particular purpose. Said goods being sold in their present condition "as is" and "where is."

Signed this _____ day of _____ , _____ (year).

In the presence of:

_____	_____
Witness' Signature	Seller's Signature
_____	_____
Print Name of Witness	Address of Seller
_____	_____
Address of Witness	Buyer's Signature
	_____
	Address of Buyer

159

CERTIFICATE OF CORPORATE RESOLUTION

_____
(Corporation)

I,   , Clerk or Secretary of   ,
(Corporation) do hereby certify that at a duly constituted meeting of the Directors and/or stockholders of the Corporation held at offices of the Corporation on   ,
(year), it was upon motion duly made and seconded, that it be

VOTED: (Describe approved corporate action)

It was upon motion made and seconded that it be further

VOTED: That   (individual) as   (officership) of the Corporation be empowered and directed to execute, deliver and accept, in the name and on behalf of the company, any and all documents reasonably required to accomplish the foregoing vote, all on such terms and conditions as deemed to be in the best interests of the Corporation.

I further certify that the foregoing votes are in full force without recision, modification or amendment.

Signed this   day of   ,   (year).

A TRUE RECORD

ATTEST

_____
Secretary/Clerk

160

CERTIFICATE OF CORPORATE RESOLUTION
TO PLEDGE CORPORATE ASSETS AS COLLATERAL

(Corporation)

I,   , Clerk or Secretary of   ,
(Corporation) do hereby certify that at a duly constituted meeting of the Directors and/or
stockholders of the Corporation held at offices of the Corporation on
(year), it was upon motion duly made and seconded, that it be

VOTED: To execute and deliver to
(Creditor) a security agreement and financing agreement pledging all, or part of the
Corporation's assets to said Creditor as collateral security for any indebtedness now or
hereinafter due, as more particularly set forth in said security agreement.

It was upon motion made and seconded that it be further

VOTED: That   (individual) as   (officership)
of the Corporation be empowered and directed to execute, deliver and accept in the name
and on behalf of the company, any and all documents reasonably required to accomplish
the foregoing vote, all on such terms and conditions as deemed to be in the best interests of
the Corporation.

I further certify that the foregoing votes are in full force without recision,
modification or amendment.

Signed this   day of   ,   (year).

A TRUE RECORD

ATTEST

_____
Secretary/Clerk

161

Bylaws

of

_____

adopted_____

BYLAWS
OF

_____

ARTICLE I
OFFICES

The principal office of the Corporation in the State of   shall be located in   , County of   . The Corporation may have such other offices, either within or without the State of   , as the Board of Directors may designate or as the business of the Corporation may require from time to time.

ARTICLE II
SHAREHOLDERS

SECTION 1. <u>Annual Meeting</u>. The annual meeting of the shareholders shall be held on the   day in the month of   in each year, beginning with the year   , at the hour of   o'clock   .m., for the purpose of electing Directors and for the transaction of such other business as may come before the meeting. If the day fixed for the annual meeting shall be a legal holiday in the State of   , such meeting shall be held on the next succeeding business day. If the election of Directors shall not be held on the day designated herein for any annual meeting of the shareholders, or at any adjournment thereof, the Board of Directors shall cause the election to be held at a special meeting of the shareholders as soon thereafter as conveniently may be.

SECTION 2. <u>Special Meetings</u>. Special meetings of the shareholders, for any purpose or purposes, unless otherwise prescribed by statute, may be called by the President or by the Board of Directors, and shall be called by the President at the request of the holders of not less than   percent (%) of all the outstanding shares of the Corporation entitled to vote at the meeting.

SECTION 3. <u>Place of Meeting</u>. The Board of Directors may designate any place, either within or without the State of   , unless otherwise prescribed by statute, as the place of meeting for any annual meeting or for any special meeting. A waiver of notice signed by all shareholders entitled to vote at a meeting may designate any place, either within or without the State of   , unless otherwise prescribed by statute, as the place for the holding of such meeting. If no designation is made, the place of meeting shall be the principal office of the Corporation.

SECTION 4. <u>Notice of Meeting</u>. Written notice stating the place, day and hour of the meeting and, in case of a special meeting, the purpose or purposes for which the meeting is called, shall unless otherwise prescribed by statute, be delivered not less than (   )   nor more than (   )   days before the date of the meeting, to each shareholder of record entitled to vote at such meeting. If mailed, such notice shall be deemed to be delivered when deposited in the United States Mail, addressed to the shareholder at his address as it appears on the stock transfer books of the Corporation, with postage thereon prepaid.

SECTION 5. Closing of Transfer Books or Fixing of Record. For the purpose of determining shareholders entitled to notice of or to vote at any meeting of shareholders or any adjournment thereof, or shareholders entitled to receive payment of any dividend, or in order to make a determination of shareholders for any other proper purpose, the Board of Directors of the Corporation may provide that the stock transfer books shall be closed for a stated period, but not to exceed in any case fifty (50) days. If the stock transfer books shall be closed for the purpose of determining shareholders entitled to notice of or to vote at a meeting of share-holders, such books shall be closed for at least (   ) days immediately preceding such meeting. In lieu of closing the stock transfer books, the Board of Directors may fix in advance a date as the record date for any such determination of shareholders, such date in any case to be not more than (   )   days and, in case of a meeting of shareholders, not less than (   )   days, prior to the date on which the particular action requiring such determination of shareholders is to be taken. If the stock transfer books are not closed and no record date is fixed for the determination of shareholders entitled to notice of or to vote at a meeting of shareholders, or shareholders entitled to receive payment of a dividend, the date on which notice of the meeting is mailed or the date on which the resolution of the Board of Directors declaring such dividend is adopted, as the case may be, shall be the record date for such determination of shareholders. When a determination of shareholders entitled to vote at any meeting of shareholders has been made as provided in this section, such determination shall apply to any adjournment thereof.

SECTION 6. Voting Lists. The officer or agent having charge of the stock transfer books for shares of the corporation shall make a complete list of the shareholders entitled to vote at each meeting of shareholders or any adjournment thereof, arranged in alphabetical order, with the address of and the number of shares held by each. Such list shall be produced and kept open at the time and place of the meeting and shall be subject to the inspection of any shareholder during the whole time of the meeting for the purposes thereof.

SECTION 7. Quorum. A majority of the outstanding shares of the Corporation entitled to vote, represented in person or by proxy, shall constitute a quorum at a meeting of shareholders. If less than a majority of the outstanding shares are represented at a meeting, a majority of the shares so represented may adjourn the meeting from time to time without further notice. At such adjourned meeting at which a quorum shall be present or represented, any business may be transacted which might have been transacted at the meeting as originally noticed. The shareholders present at a duly organized meeting may continue to transact business until adjournment, notwithstanding the withdrawal of enough shareholders to leave less than a quorum.

SECTION 8. Proxies. At all meetings of shareholders, a shareholder may vote in person or by proxy executed in writing by the shareholder or by his duly authorized attorney-in-fact. Such proxy shall be filed with the secretary of the Corporation before or at the time of the meeting. A meeting of the Board of Directors may be had by means of a telephone conference or similar communications equipment by which all persons participating in the meeting can hear each other, and participation in a meeting under such circumstances shall constitute presence at the meeting.

SECTION 9. Voting of Shares. Each outstanding share entitled to vote shall be entitled to one vote upon each matter submitted to a vote at a meeting of shareholders.

SECTION 10. Voting of Shares by Certain Holders. Shares standing in the name of another corporation may be voted by such officer, agent or proxy as the Bylaws of such corporation may prescribe or, in the absence of such provision, as the Board of Directors of such corporation may determine.

Shares held by an administrator, executor, guardian or conservator may be voted by him, either in person or by proxy, without a transfer of such shares into his name. Shares standing in the name of a trustee may be voted by him, either in person or by proxy, but no trustee shall be entitled to vote shares held by him without a transfer of such shares into his name.

Shares standing in the name of a receiver may be voted by such receiver, and shares held by or under the control of a receiver may be voted by such receiver without the transfer thereof into his name, if authority so to do be contained in an appropriate order of the court by which such receiver was appointed.

A shareholder whose shares are pledged shall be entitled to vote such shares until the shares have been transferred into the name of the pledgee, and thereafter the pledgee shall be entitled to vote the shares so transferred.

Shares of its own stock belonging to the Corporation shall not be voted, directly or indirectly, at any meeting, and shall not be counted in determining the total number of outstanding shares at any given time.

SECTION 11. Informal Action by Shareholders. Unless otherwise provided by law, any action required to be taken at a meeting of the shareholders, or any other action which may be taken at a meeting of the shareholders, may be taken without a meeting if a consent in writing, setting forth the action so taken, shall be signed by all of the shareholders entitled to vote with respect to the subject matter thereof.

ARTICLE III
BOARD OF DIRECTORS

SECTION 1. General Powers. The business and affairs of the Corporation shall be managed by its Board of Directors.

SECTION 2. Number, Tenure and Qualifications. The number of directors of the Corporation shall be fixed by the Board of Directors, but in no event shall be less than ( ). Each director shall hold office until the next annual meeting of shareholders and until his successor shall have been elected and qualified.

SECTION 3. Regular Meetings. A regular meeting of the Board of Directors shall be held without other notice than this Bylaw immediately after, and at the same place as, the annual meeting of shareholders. The Board of Directors may provide, by resolution, the time and place for the holding of additional regular meetings without notice other than such resolution.

SECTION 4. Special Meetings. Special meetings of the Board of Directors may be called by or at the request of the President or any two directors. The person or persons authorized to call special meetings of the Board of Directors may fix the place for holding any special meeting of the Board of Directors called by them.

SECTION 5. Notice. Notice of any special meeting shall be given at least one (1) day previous thereto by written notice delivered personally or mailed to each director at his business address, or by telegram. If mailed, such notice shall be deemed to be delivered when deposited in the United States Mail so addressed, with postage thereon prepaid. If notice be given by telegram, such notice shall be deemed to be delivered when the telegram is delivered to the telegraph company. Any directors may waive notice of any meeting. The attendance of a director at a meeting shall constitute a waiver of notice of such meeting.

except where a director attends a meeting for the express purpose of objecting to the transaction of any business because the meeting is not lawfully called or convened.

SECTION 6. Quorum. A majority of the number of directors fixed by Section 2 of this Article III shall constitute a quorum for the transaction of business at any meeting of the Board of Directors, but if less than such majority is present at a meeting, a majority of the directors present may adjourn the meeting from time to time without further notice.

SECTION 7. Manner of Acting. The act of the majority of the directors present at a meeting at which a quorum is present shall be the act of the Board of Directors.

SECTION 8. Action Without a Meeting. Any action that may be taken by the Board of Directors at a meeting may be taken without a meeting if a consent in writing, setting forth the action so to be taken, shall be signed before such action by all of the directors.

SECTION 9. Vacancies. Any vacancy occurring in the Board of Directors may be filled by the affirmative vote of a majority of the remaining directors though less than a quorum of the Board of Directors, unless otherwise provided by law. A director elected to fill a vacancy shall be elected for the unexpired term of his predecessor in office. Any directorship to be filled by reason of an increase in the number of directors may be filled by election by the Board of Directors for a term of office continuing only until the next election of directors by the shareholders.

SECTION 10. Compensation. By resolution of the Board of Directors, each director may be paid his expenses, if any, of attendance at each meeting of the Board of Directors, and may be paid a stated salary as director or a fixed sum for attendance at each meeting of the Board of Directors or both. No such payment shall preclude any director from serving the Corporation in any other capacity and receiving compensation therefor.

SECTION 11. Presumption of Assent. A director of the Corporation who is present at a meeting of the Board of Directors at which action on any corporate matter is taken shall be presumed to have assented to the action taken unless his dissent shall be entered in the minutes of the meeting or unless he shall file his written dissent to such action with the person acting as the Secretary of the meeting before the adjournment thereof, or shall forward such dissent by registered mail to the Secretary of the Corporation immediately after the adjournment of the meeting. Such right to dissent shall not apply to a director who voted in favor of such action.

ARTICLE IV
OFFICERS

SECTION 1. Number. The officers of the Corporation shall be a President, one or more Vice Presidents, a Secretary and a Treasurer, each of whom shall be elected by the Board of Directors. Such other officers and assistant officers as may be deemed necessary may be elected or appointed by the Board of Directors, including a Chairman of the Board. In its discretion, the Board of Directors may leave unfilled for any such period as it may determine any office except those of President and Secretary. Any two or more offices may be held by the same person, except for the offices of President and Secretary which may not be held by the same person. Officers may be directors or shareholders of the Corporation.

SECTION 2. Election and Term of Office. The officers of the Corporation to be elected by the Board of Directors shall be elected annually by the Board of Directors at the first meeting of the Board of Directors held after each annual meeting of the shareholders. If the election of officers shall not be held at such meeting, such election shall be held as soon thereafter as conveniently may be. Each officer shall hold office until his successor shall have been duly elected and shall have qualified, or until his death, or until he shall resign or shall have been removed in the manner hereinafter provided.

SECTION 3. Removal. Any officer or agent may be removed by the Board of Directors whenever, in its judgement, the best interests of the Corporation will be served thereby, but such removal shall be without prejudice to the contract rights, if any, of the person so removed. Election or appointment of an officer or agent shall not of itself create contract rights, and such appointment shall be terminable at will.

SECTION 4. Vacancies. A vacancy in any office because of death, resignation, removal, disqualification or otherwise, may be filled by the Board of Directors for the unexpired portion of the term.

SECTION 5. President. The President shall be the principal executive officer of the Corporation and, subject to the control of the Board of Directors, shall in general supervise and control all of the business and affairs of the Corporation. He shall, when present, preside at all meetings of the shareholders and of the Board of Directors, unless there is a Chairman of the Board, in which case the Chairman shall preside. He may sign, with the Secretary or any other proper officer of the Corporation thereunto authorized by the Board of Directors, certificates for shares of the Corporation, any deeds, mortgages, bonds, contracts, or other instruments which the Board of Directors has authorized to be executed, except in cases where the signing and execution thereof shall be expressly delegated by the Board of Directors or by these Bylaws to some other officer or agent of the Corporation, or shall be required by law to be otherwise signed or executed; and in general shall perform all duties incident to the office of President and such other duties as may be prescribed by the Board of Directors from time to time.

SECTION 6. Vice President. In the absence of the President or in event of his death, inability or refusal to act, the Vice President shall perform the duties of the President, and when so acting, shall have all the powers of and be subject to all the restrictions upon the President. The Vice President shall perform such other duties as from time to time may be assigned to him by the President or by the Board of Directors. If there is more than one Vice President, each Vice President shall succeed to the duties of the President in order of rank as determined by the Board of Directors. If no such rank has been determined, then each Vice President shall succeed to the duties of the President in order of date of election, the earliest date having the first rank.

SECTION 7. Secretary. The Secretary shall: (a) keep the minutes of the proceedings of the shareholders and of the Board of Directors in one or more minute books provided for that purpose; (b) see that all notices are duly given in accordance with the provisions of these Bylaws or as required by law; (c) be custodian of the corporate records and of the seal of the Corporation and see that the seal of the Corporation is affixed to all documents, the execution of which on behalf of the Corporation under its seal is duly authorized; (d) keep a register of the post office address of each shareholder which shall be furnished to the Secretary by such shareholder; (e) sign with the President certificates for shares of the Corporation, the issuance of which shall have been authorized by resolution of the Board of Directors; (f) have general charge of the stock transfer books of the Corporation; and (g) in general perform all duties incident to the office of the Secretary and such other duties as from time to time may be assigned to him by the President or by the Board of Directors.

SECTION 8. Treasurer. The Treasurer shall: (a) have charge and custody of and be responsible for all funds and securities of the Corporation; (b) receive and give receipts for moneys due and payable to the Corporation from any source what-soever, and deposit all such moneys in the name of the Corporation in such banks, trust companies or other depositories as shall be selected in accordance with the provisions of Article VI of these Bylaws; and (c) in general perform all of the duties incident to the office of Treasurer and such other duties as from time to time may be assigned to him by the President or by the Board of Directors. If required by the Board of Directors, the Treasurer shall give a bond for the faithful discharge of his duties in such sum and with such sureties as the Board of Directors shall determine.

SECTION 9. Salaries. The salaries of the officers shall be fixed from time to time by the Board of Directors, and no officer shall be prevented from receiving such salary by reason of the fact that he is also a director of the Corporation.

ARTICLE V
INDEMNITY

The Corporation shall indemnify its directors, officers and employees as follows:

(a) Every director, officer, or employee of the Corporation shall be indemnified by the Corporation against all expenses and liabilities, including counsel fees, reasonably incurred by or imposed upon him in connection with any proceeding to which he may be made a party, or in which he may become involved, by reason of his being or having been a director, officer, employee or agent of the Corporation or is or was serving at the request of the Corporation as a director, officer, employee or agent of the corporation, partnership, joint venture, trust or enterprise, or any settlement thereof, whether or not he is a director, officer, employee or agent at the time such expenses are incurred, except in such cases wherein the director, officer, or employee is adjudged guilty of willful misfeasance or malfeasance in the performance of his duties; provided that in the event of a settlement the indemnification herein shall apply only when the Board of Directors approves such settlement and reimbursement as being for the best interests of the Corporation.

(b) The Corporation shall provide to any person who is or was a director, officer, employee, or agent of the Corporation or is or was serving at the request of the Corporation as a director, officer, employee or agent of the corporation, partnership, joint venture, trust or enterprise, the indemnity against expenses of suit, litigation or other proceedings which is specifically permissible under applicable law.

(c) The Board of Directors may, in its discretion, direct the purchase of liability insurance by way of implementing the provisions of this Article V.

ARTICLE VI
CONTRACTS, LOANS, CHECKS AND DEPOSITS

SECTION 1. Contracts. The Board of Directors may authorize any officer or officers, agent or agents, to enter into any contract or execute and deliver any instrument in the name of and on behalf of the Corporation, and such authority may be general or confined to specific instances.

SECTION 2. Loans. No loans shall be contracted on behalf of the Corporation and no evidences of indebtedness shall be issued in its name unless authorized by a resolution of the Board of Directors. Such authority may be general or confined to specific instances.

SECTION 3. Checks, Drafts, etc. All checks, drafts or other orders for the payment of money, notes or other evidences of indebtedness issued in the name of the Corporation, shall be signed by such officer or officers, agent or agents of the Corporation and in such manner as shall from time to time be determined by resolution of the Board of Directors.

SECTION 4. Deposits. All funds of the Corporation not otherwise employed shall be deposited from time to time to the credit of the Corporation in such banks, trust companies or other depositories as the Board of Directors may select.

ARTICLE VII
CERTIFICATES FOR SHARES AND THEIR TRANSFER

SECTION 1. Certificates for Shares. Certificates representing shares of the Corporation shall be in such form as shall be determined by the Board of Directors. Such certificates shall be signed by the President and by the Secretary or by such other officers authorized by law and by the Board of Directors so to do, and sealed with the corporate seal. All certificates for shares shall be consecutively numbered or otherwise identified. The name and address of the person to whom the shares represented thereby are issued, with the number of shares and date of issue, shall be entered on the stock transfer books of the Corporation. All certificates surrendered to the Corporation for transfer shall be cancelled and no new certificate shall be issued until the former certificate for a like number of shares shall have been surrendered and cancelled, except that in case of a lost, destroyed or mutilated certificate, a new one may be issued therefor upon such terms and indemnity to the Corporation as the Board of Directors may prescribe.

SECTION 2. Transfer of Shares. Transfer of shares of the Corporation shall be made only on the stock transfer books of the Corporation by the holder of record thereof or by his legal representative, who shall furnish proper evidence of authority to transfer, or by his attorney thereunto authorized by power of attorney duly executed and filed with the Secretary of the Corporation, and on surrender for cancellation of the certificate for such shares. The person in whose name shares stand on the books of the Corporation shall be deemed by the Corporation to be the owner thereof for all purposes. Provided, however, that upon any action undertaken by the shareholders to elect S Corporation status pursuant to Section 1362 of the Internal Revenue Code and upon any shareholders agreement thereto restricting the transfer of said shares so as to disqualify said S Corporation status, said restriction on transfer shall be made a part of the bylaws so long as said agreement is in force and effect.

ARTICLE VIII
FISCAL YEAR

The fiscal year of the Corporation shall begin on the   day of
and end on the   day of   of each year.

ARTICLE IX
DIVIDENDS

The Board of Directors may from time to time declare, and the Corporation may pay, dividends on its outstanding shares in the manner and upon the terms and conditions provided by law and its Articles of Incorporation.

ARTICLE X
CORPORATE SEAL

The Board of Directors shall provide a corporate seal which shall be circular in form and shall have inscribed thereon the name of the Corporation and the state of incorporation and the words, "Corporate Seal".

ARTICLE XI
WAIVER OF NOTICE

Unless otherwise provided by law, whenever any notice is required to be given to any shareholder or director of the Corporation under the provisions of these Bylaws or under the provisions of the Articles of Incorporation or under the provisions of the applicable Business Corporation Act, a waiver thereof in writing, signed by the person or persons entitled to such notice, whether before or after the time stated therein, shall be deemed equivalent to the giving of such notice.

ARTICLE XII
AMENDMENTS

These Bylaws may be altered, amended or repealed and new Bylaws may be adopted by the Board of Directors at any regular or special meeting of the Board of Directors.

The above Bylaws are certified to have been adopted by the Board of Directors of the Corporation on the   day of   ,   (year).

_____

Secretary

General Partnership Agreement

of

_____

adopted _____

GENERAL PARTNERSHIP AGREEMENT

AGREEMENT by and between the Undersigned

("Partners").

1.   **Name**. The name of the partnership is:

2.   **Partners**. The names of the initial partners are:

3.   **Place of Business**. The principal place of business of the partnership is:

4.   **Nature of Business**. The partnership shall generally engage in the following business:

5.   **Duration**. The partnership shall commence business on   and shall continue until terminated by this agreement, or by operation of law.

6.   **Contribution of Capital**. The partners shall contribute capital in proportionate shares as follows:

Partner	Capital	Partnership Shares
_____	_____	_____
_____	_____	_____
_____	_____	_____
_____	_____	_____

172

7. **Allocation of Depreciation or Gain or Loss on Contributed Property.** The partners understand that, for income tax purposes, the partnership's adjusted basis of some of the contributed property differs from fair market value at which the property was accepted by the partnership. However, the partners intend that the general allocation rule of the Internal Revenue Code shall apply, and that the depreciation or gain or loss arising with respect to this property shall be allocated proportionately between the partners, as allocated in Paragraph 6 above, in determining the taxable income or loss of the partnership and the distributive share of each partner, in the same manner as if such property had been purchased by the partnership at a cost equal to the adjusted tax basis.

8. **Capital Accounts.** An individual capital account shall be maintained for each partner. The capital of each partner shall consist of that partner's original contribution of capital, as described in Paragraph 6, and increased by additional capital contributions and decreased by distributions in reduction of partnership capital and reduced by his/her share of partnership losses, if these losses are charged to the capital accounts.

9. **Drawing Accounts.** An individual drawing account shall be maintained for each partner. All withdrawals by a partner shall be charged to his drawing account. Withdrawals shall be limited to amounts unanimously agreed to by the partners.

10. **Salaries.** No partner shall receive any salary for services rendered to the partnership except as specifically and first approved by each of the partners.

11. **Loans by Partners.** If a majority of partners consent, any partner may lend money to the partnership at an interest and terms rate agreed in writing, at the time said loan is made.

12. **Profits and Losses.** Net profits of the partnership shall be divided proportionately between the partners, and the net losses shall be borne proportionately as follows:

Partner	Proportion
_____	_____
_____	_____
_____	_____

13. **Management.** The partners shall have equal rights and control in the management of the partnership.

14. **Books of Accounts.** The partnership shall maintain adequate accounting records. All books, records, and accounts of the partnership shall be open at all times to inspection by all partners, or their designated representatives.

15. **Accounting Basis.** The books of account shall be kept on a cash basis.

16. **Fiscal Year.** The books of account shall be kept on a fiscal year basis, commencing January 1 and ending December 31, and shall be closed and balanced at the end of each year.

17. **Annual Audit.** The books of account shall be audited as of the close of each fiscal year by an accountant chosen by the partners.

18. **Banking.** All funds of the partnership shall be deposited in the name of the partnership into such checking or savings accounts as designated by the partners.

19. **Death or Incapacity.** The death or incapacity of a partner shall cause an immediate dissolution of the partnership.

20. **Election of Remaining Partner to Continue Business.** In the event of the retirement, death, incapacity, or insanity of a partner, the remaining partners shall have the right to continue the business of the partnership, either by themselves or in conjunction with any other person or persons they may select, but they shall pay to the retiring partner, or to the legal representatives of the deceased or incapacitated partner, the value of his or her interest in the partnership.

21. **Valuation of Partner's Interest.** The value of the interest of a retiring, incapacitated, deceased, or insane partner shall be the sum of (a) the partner's capital account, (b) any unpaid loans due the partner, and (c) the partner's proportionate share of the accrued net profits remaining undistributed in his drawing account. No value for goodwill shall be included in determining the value of a partner's interest, unless specifically agreed in advance by the partners.

22. **Payment of Purchase Price.** The value of the partner's interest shall be paid without interest to the retiring partner, or to the legal representative of the deceased, incapacitated or insane partner, in   (   ) monthly installments, commencing on the first day of the second month after the effective date of the purchase.

23.   **Termination.** In the event that the remaining partner does not elect to purchase the interest of the retiring, deceased, incapacitated, or insane partner, or in the event the partners mutually agree to dissolve, the partnership shall terminate and the partners shall proceed with reasonable promptness to liquidate the business of the partnership. The assets of the partnership shall first be used to pay or provide for all debts of the partnership. Thereafter, all money remaining undistributed in the drawing accounts shall be paid to the partners. Then the remaining assets shall be divided proportionately as follows:

Partner   Percentage

_____   _____

_____   _____

_____   _____

24.   This agreement shall be binding upon and inure to the benefit of the parties, their successors, assigns and personal representatives.

Signed this   day of   ,   (year).

_____   _____
Partner   Partner

_____   _____
Partner   Partner

_____   _____
Witness   Partner

State of   }
County of
On   before me,   , appeared
                              , personally known to me (or proved to me on the basis of satisfactory evidence) to be the person(s) whose name(s) is/are subscribed to the within instrument and acknowledged to me that he/she/they executed the same in his/her/their authorized capacity(ies), and that by his/her/their signature(s) on the instrument the person(s), or the entity upon behalf of which the person(s) acted, executed the instrument.

WITNESS my hand and official seal.

Signature_____

                                        Affiant _____Known_____Produced ID

(Seal)   Type of ID _____

Limited Partnership Agreement

of

_____

adopted _____

LIMITED PARTNERSHIP AGREEMENT
FOR _____

THIS LIMITED PARTNERSHIP AGREEMENT (the Agreement) is made and entered into as of

the _____ day of _____, _____(year) by and among:

_____, as the General Partner

and _____

_____, as the limited partners,

and each individual or business entity as shall be subsequently admitted as a Partner. These indi-

viduals and/or business entities shall be known as and referred to as "Partners."

WHEREAS, the parties have formed a Limited Partnership named above through their initial reg-

istered agent _____ pursuant to the laws of the State of

_____. NOW, in consideration of the conditions and mutual covenants

contained herein, and for good and valuable consideration, the parties agree upon the following

terms and conditions:

ARTICLE I: COMPANY FORMATION

1. The Partners hereby form and organize the company as a Limited Partnership subject to the pro-

visions of the _____Limited Partnership Act in effect as of this date. A

Certificate of Organization shall be filed forthwith with the _____Secretary of State.

2. The Partners agree to execute this Agreement and hereby acknowledge for good and valuable

consideration receipt thereof. It is the intention of the Partners that this Partnership Agreement, or

as may be amended, shall be the sole agreement of the parties.

In the event any provision of this Limited Partnership Agreement is prohibited or rendered inef-

fective under the laws of_____, this Agreement shall be considered amend-

ed to conform to the_____ Act as set forth in the Code of _____.

The invalidity of any provision of this Agreement shall not affect the subsequent validity of any

other provisions of this Agreement.

3. NAME. The name of the Limited Partnership shall be_____

_____. The business of the company shall be conducted under that name or such trade or fictitious names as the Partners may determine.

4. DATE OF FORMATION. This Agreement shall become effective upon its filing with and acceptance by the appropriate state agency.

5. REGISTERED AGENT AND OFFICE. The Limited Partnership's initial registered agent and registered office shall be _____

_____. The Partners may change the registered agent or registered office at any time, by filing the necessary documents with the appropriate state agency. Should the Partners fail to act in this regard, the General Partner file such notice of change in registered agent or registered office.

6. TERM. The limited Partner shall continue for a period of thirty (30) years from the date of formation unless:

a)   The term extended by amendment to the Agreement. Partners shall have the right to continue the business of the Partnership and may exercise that right by the unanimous vote of the remaining Partners within ninety (90) days after the occurrence of the event described below.

b)   The Partnership is dissolved by a majority vote of the Partners.

c)   The death, resignation, expulsion, retirement, bankruptcy, incapacity or any other event that terminates the continued Partnership of a Partner.

d)   Any event which makes it unlawful for the business of the Partnership to be carried on by the Partners.

e)   Any other event that causes the dissolution of a Limited Partnership under the laws of the state of _____ .

ARTICLE II: BUSINESS PURPOSE

It is the purpose of the Limited Partnership to engage in_____

_____. The foregoing purposes and activities will be interpreted as examples only and not as limitations, and nothing therein shall be deemed as prohibiting the Partnership from extending its activities to any related or otherwise permissible lawful business purpose which may become necessary, profitable or desirable for the furtherance of the Partnerships objectives expressed above.

ARTICLE III: CAPITAL CONTRIBUTIONS

1. INITIAL CONTRIBUTIONS. Each Partner shall contribute to the Partnership certain capital prior to or simultaneously with, the execution of this Agreement. Each Partner shall have made initial capital contributions in the following amounts:

Name of Partner	Value of Capital Contribution
_____	_____
_____	_____
_____	_____
_____	_____

No interest shall accrue on initial capital contributions.

2. ADDITIONAL CAPITAL CONTRIBUTIONS. If the General Partner decides that additional capital contributions are necessary for operating expenses or to meet other obligations, notice must be sent to each Partner setting forth each Partner's share of the total contribution. Such notice must be in writing and delivered to the Partner at least ten (10) business days prior to the date the contribution is due. Any such additional capital contribution is strictly voluntary and any such commitment is to be considered a loan of capital by the Partner to the Limited Partnership. Such additional capital contribution does not in any way increase the percentage of Partnership interest. This loan shall bear interest at _____ points above the current prime rate. Any loan under this subsection shall be paid in full before distributions are made under Article IV.

3. THIRD PARTY BENEFICIARIES. Nothing in the foregoing sections is intended to benefit any creditor or third party to whom obligations are owed without the expressed written consent of the Partnership or any of its Partners.

4. CAPITAL ACCOUNTS. A capital account shall be established by the Partnership for each Partner. The capital account shall consist of:

   a) The amount of the Partner's Capital Contributions to the Partnership, including the fair market value of any property so contributed to the Partnership or distributed by the Partnership to the Partner.

   b) Member's share of net profits or net losses and of any separate allocations of income, gain (including unrealized gain), loss or deduction. The maintenance of capital accounts shall at all times be in accordance with the requirements of state law.

5. ADDITIONAL PROVISIONS:

   a) Capital accounts shall be non-interest bearing accounts.

   b) Until the dissolution of the Partnership, no Partner may receive Partnership property in return for Capital contributions.

   c) The liability of any Partner for the losses or obligations incurred by the Partnership shall be limited to: Payment of capital contributions when due, *pro rata* share of undistributed Partnership assets and only to the extent required by law, any previous distributions to that Partner from the Partnership.

ARTICLE IV: PROFITS, LOSSES, ALLOCATIONS AND DISTRIBUTIONS

1. ALLOCATIONS. Net profits, losses, gains, deductions and credits from operations and financing shall be distributed among the Partners in proportion to their respective interest and at such time as shall be determined by the Partners.

2. DISTRIBUTIONS. The General Partner may make distributions annually or more frequently if there is excess cash on hand after providing for appropriate expenses and liabilities. Such interim distributions are allocated to each Partner according to the percentage of Partnership interest.

ARTICLE V: Management

1. MANAGERS. The names and addresses of General Partners are:

_____

_____

_____

The General Partners shall make decisions regarding the usual affairs of the Limited Partnership. A majority vote of the Partners shall name successors as the General Partners deem necessary and who is responsible for all management decisions and undertakings.

2. NUMBER OF GENERAL PARTNERS. The Partners may elect one, but not fewer than one, General Partner.

3. TERM OF OFFICE. The term of office is not contractual but continues until:

a) A fixed term of office, as designated by the Partnership, expires.

b) The General Partner is removed with or without cause, by a majority vote of the Partnership.

c) The dissociation of such General Partner.

4. AUTHORITY OF GENERAL PARTNER. Only the General Partner and authorized agents shall have the power to bind the Partnership. Each General Partner is authorized on the Partnership's behalf to:

a) Purchase, or otherwise acquire, sell, develop, pledge, convey, exchange, lease or otherwise dispose of Partnership assets wherever located.

b) Initiate, prosecute and defend any proceeding on behalf of the Partnership.

c) Incur and secure liabilities and obligations on behalf of the Partnership.

d) Lend, invest or re-invest Partnership assets as security for repayment. Money may be lent to Partners, employees and agents of the Partnership.

e) Appoint officers and agents, and hire employees. It is also the province of the General Partner to define duties and establish levels of compensation. Management compensation will be determined by majority Partner vote.

f) Execute and deliver all contracts, conveyances, assignments, leases, subleases, franchise and licensing agreements, promissory notes, loans, security agreements or any other kind relating to Partnership business.

g) Establish pensions, trusts, life insurance, incentive plans or any variation thereof, for the benefit of any or all current or former employees, Partners and agents of the Partnership.

h) Make charitable donations in the Partnership's name.

i) Seek advice from limited Partners, although, such advice need not be heeded.

j) Supply, upon the proper request of any Partner, information about the Partnership or any of its activities including but not limited to, access to Partnership records for the purpose of inspecting and copying Partnership books, records and materials in the possession of the General Partner. The Requesting Partner shall be responsible for any expenses incurred in the exercise of these rights set forth in this document.

5. STANDARD OF CARE AND EXCULPATION. Any General Partner must refrain from engaging in grossly negligent, reckless or intentional misconduct. Any act or omission of a General Partner that results in loss or damage to the Partnership, if done in good faith, shall not make the General Partner liable to the Partners.

6. INDEMNIFICATION. The Partnership shall indemnify its General Partner, employees and agents as follows:

a) Every General Partner, agent, or employee of the Partnership shall be indemnified by the Partnership against all expenses and liabilities, including counsel fees reasonably incurred by him in connection with any proceeding to which he may become involved, by reason of his being or having been a General Partner of the Partnership, except in such cases wherein the General Partner, agent or employee is adjudged guilty of willful misfeasance or malfeasance in the performance of his duties; provided that in the event of a settlement the indemnification herein shall apply only when the General Partner approves such settlement and reimbursement as being in the best interests of the Partnership.

b) The Partnership shall provide to any person who is or was a General Partner, employee, or agent of the Partnership or is or was serving at the request of the Partnership as General Partner, employee, or agent of the Partnership, the indemnity against expenses of suit, litigation or other proceedings which is specifically permissible under applicable law.

ARTICLE VI: TAX AND ACCOUNTING MATTERS

1. BANK ACCOUNTS. General Partner shall establish bank accounts, deposit Partnership funds in those accounts and make disbursements from those accounts.

2. ACCOUNTING METHOD. The cash method of accounting shall be the accounting method used to keep records of receipts and disbursements.

3. YEARS. The fiscal and tax years of the Partnership shall be chosen by the General Partner.

4. ACCOUNTANT. An independent accountant shall be selected by the General Partner.

ARTICLE VII: PARTNER DISSOCIATION

1. Upon the first occurrence of any of the following events, a person shall cease to be a Partner of the Partnership:

  a) Bankruptcy of the Partner.

  b) Death or court-ordered adjudication of incapacity of the Partner.

  c) Withdrawal of a Partner with the consent of a majority vote of the remaining Partnership.

  d) Dissolution and winding up of any non-corporate Partner, including the termination of a trust.

  e) Filing a Certificate of Dissolution by a corporate Partner.

  f) Complete liquidation of an estate's interest in the partnership.

  g) Expulsion of the Partner with the majority consent of the remaining Partnership.

  h) Expiration of the term specified in Article I, section 6.

2. OPTION TO PURCHASE INTEREST. In the event of dissociation of a Partner, the Partnership shall have the right to purchase the former Partner's interest at current fair market value.

ARTICLE VIII: DISPOSITION OF PARTNERSHIP INTERESTS

1. PROHIBITIONS.

    a) No Partnership interest, be it a sale, assignment, exchange, transfer, mortgage, pledge or grant, shall be disposed of if the disposition would result in the dissolution of the Partnership without full compliance with all appropriate state and federal laws.

    b) No Partner may in any way alienate all or part of his Partnership interest in the Partnership be it through assignment, conveyance, encumbrance or sale, without the prior written consent of the majority of the remaining Partners. Such consent may be given, withheld or delayed as the remaining Partners see fit.

2. PERMISSIONS. A Partner may assign his Partnership interest in the Partnership subject to the provisions in this article. The assignment of Partnership interest does not in itself entitle the assignee to participate in the management of the Partnership nor is the assignee entitled to become a Partner of the Partnership. The assignee is not a substitute Partner but only an assignee of Partnership interest and as such, is entitled to receive only the income and distributions the assigning Partner would have otherwise received.

3. SUBSTITUTE PARTNERSHIP. Only upon the unanimous consent of the remaining Partners may an assignee of a Partnership interest become a substitute Partner and be entitled to all rights associated with the assignor. Upon such admission, the substitute Partner is subject to all restrictions and liabilities of a Partner.

ARTICLE IX: MEETINGS

1. VOTING. All Partners shall have the right to vote on all of the following:

    a) The dissolution of the Partnership.

    b) The merger of the Partnership.

c) Any transaction involving any potential conflict of interest.

d) An amendment to the Articles of Organization or to the Limited Partnership Agreement.

e) The transfer or disposition of all Partnership assets outside the ordinary course of business.

2. REQUIRED VOTE. Unless a greater vote is required by statute or the Articles of Organization, an affirmative vote of the majority of the Partnership shall be required.

3. MEETINGS.

a) The General Partner(s) shall hold an annual meeting at a time and place of their choosing.

b) Special meetings of the Partnership may be called at any time by the General Partner(s) or by at least ten (10%) of the Partnership interest of all Partners. Written notice of such meeting must be provided at least sixty (60) business days prior and not later than ten (10) days before the date of the meeting. A Partner may elect to participate in any meeting via telephone.

4. CONSENT. In the absence of an annual or special meeting and in the absence of a vote, any action required to be taken may be permitted with the written consent of the Partners having not less than the minimum number of votes required to authorize such action at a meeting.

ARTICLE X: DISSOLUTION AND TERMINATION

In the event a dissolution event occurs the remaining Partnership shall have the option to elect to continue the Partnership as defined by Article I, section 6.

1. MERGER. In the event the election to continue the Partnership following a dissolution event is not obtained, a majority vote of the remaining Partners may elect to reconstitute the Partnership through merger with and into another Limited Partnership pursuant to applicable state law.

2. WINDING UP. If the Partners do not elect to continue the Partnership or reconstitute it, the General Partner or other person selected by a majority vote of the Partnership shall wind up the Partnership.

3. FINAL DISTRIBUTIONS. After all Partnership assets have been liquidated and all Partnership debts have been paid, the proceeds of such liquidation shall be distributed to the Partners in

accordance with their capital account balance. Liquidation proceeds shall be paid within _____ days of the end of the Partnership's taxable year or, if later, within _____ days after the date of liquidation.

4. DISSOLUTION. Upon completion of the winding up period, the General Partner or other person selected shall file with the Secretary of State the Certificate of Dissolution or its equivalent and any other appropriate documents as required by law.

IN WITNESS WHEREOF, the parties hereto make and execute this Agreement on the dates set below their names, to be effective on the date first above written.

Signed and Agreed this _____ day of _____ , _____(year).

By

General Partner: _____

Limited Partner: _____

Limited Partner: _____

Limited Partner: _____

Operating Agreement

of

_____

adopted_____

LIMITED LIABILITY COMPANY OPERATING AGREEMENT
FOR_____

THIS LIMITED LIABILITY COMPANY OPERATING AGREEMENT (the Agreement) is made

and entered into as of the _____day of_____, _____(year) by and among:

_____

_____

_____

and each individual or business entity as shall be subsequently admitted to the Company. These

individuals and/or business entities shall be known as and referred to as "Members" and individ-

ually as a "Member." WHEREAS, the parties have formed a Limited Liability Company named

above through their initial registered agent _____ pursuant to the

laws of the State of _____. NOW, in consideration of the conditions and

mutual covenants contained herein, and for good and valuable consideration, the parties agree

upon the following terms and conditions:

ARTICLE I: COMPANY FORMATION

1. The members hereby form and organize the company as a Limited Liability Company subject

to the provisions of the _____Limited Liability Company Act in effect as

of this date. Articles of Organization shall be filed with the _____Secretary of State.

2. The members agree to execute this Operating Agreement and hereby acknowledge for good and

valuable consideration receipt thereof. It is the intention of the members that this Operating

Agreement shall be the sole source of agreement of the parties.

In the event any provision of this Operating Agreement is prohibited or rendered ineffective under

the laws of_____, this Operating Agreement shall be considered amended to

conform to the_____ Act as set forth in the Code of _____. The

invalidity of any provision of this Operating Agreement shall not affect the subsequent validity

of any other provisions of this Operating Agreement.

188

3. NAME. The name of the company shall be _____

_____. The business of the company shall be conducted under that name or such trade or fictitious names as the members may determine.

4. DATE OF FORMATION. This Operating Agreement shall become effective upon its filing with and acceptance by the appropriate state agency.

5. REGISTERED AGENT AND OFFICE. The company's initial registered agent and registered office shall be _____

_____. Managing members may change the registered agent or registered office at any time, by filing the necessary documents with the appropriate state agency. Should managing members fail to act in this regard, any member may file such notice of change in registered agent or registered office.

6. TERM. The company shall continue for a period of thirty (30) years from the date of formation unless:

a) The term is extended by amendment of the Operating Agreement. Members shall have the right to continue the business of the Company and may exercise that right by the unanimous vote of the remaining Members within ninety (90) days after the occurrence of the event described below.

b) The company is dissolved by a majority vote of the membership.

c) The death, resignation, expulsion, retirement, bankruptcy, incapacity or any other event that terminates the continued membership of a Member of the Company.

d) Any event which makes it unlawful for the business of the Company to be carried on by the Members.

e) Any other event causing the dissolution of a Limited Liability Company under the laws of the state of _____.

ARTICLE II: BUSINESS PURPOSE

It is the purpose of the Company to engage in_____
_____. The foregoing purposes and activities
will be interpreted as examples only and not as limitations, and nothing therein shall be deemed
as prohibiting the Company from extending its activities to any related or otherwise permissible
lawful business purpose which may become necessary, profitable or desirable for the furtherance
of the company objectives expressed above.

ARTICLE III: CAPITAL CONTRIBUTIONS

1. INITIAL CONTRIBUTIONS. Each Member shall contribute to the Company capital prior to
or simultaneously with, the execution of this Agreement. Each Member shall have made initial
capital contributions in the following amounts:

Name of Member	Value of Capital Contribution
_____	_____
_____	_____
_____	_____
_____	_____

No interest shall accrue on initial capital contributions.

2. ADDITIONAL CAPITAL CONTRIBUTIONS. If management decides that additional capital
contributions are necessary for operating expenses or to meet other obligations, notice must be
sent to each Member setting forth each Member's share of the total contribution. Such notice must
be in writing and delivered to the Member at least ten (10) business days prior to the date the
contribution is due. Any such additional capital contribution is strictly voluntary and any such
commitment is to be considered a loan of capital by the Member to the Company. Such additional
capital contribution does not in any way increase percentage of membership interest. This loan shall
bear interest at _____ points above the current prime rate. Any loan under this
subsection shall be paid in full before any distributions are made under Article IV.

3. THIRD PARTY BENEFICIARIES. Nothing in the foregoing sections is intended to benefit any creditor or third party to whom obligations are owed without the expressed written consent of the Company or any of its Members.

4. CAPITAL ACCOUNTS. A capital account shall be established by the Company for each Member. The capital account shall consist of:

a) The amount of the Member's Capital Contributions to the Company including the fair market value of any property so contributed to the Company or distributed by the Company to the Member.

b) Member's share of net profits or net losses and of any separate allocations of income, gain (including unrealized gain), loss or deduction. The maintenance of capital accounts shall at all times be in accordance with the requirements of state law.

5. ADDITIONAL PROVISIONS:

a) Capital accounts shall be non-interest bearing accounts.

b) Until the dissolution of the company, no Member may receive Company property in return for Capital contributions.

c) The liability of any member for the losses or obligations incurred by the Company shall be limited to: Payment of capital contributions when due, *pro rata* share of undistributed Company assets and only to the extent required by law, any previous distributions to that Member from the Company.

ARTICLE IV: PROFITS, LOSSES, ALLOCATIONS AND DISTRIBUTIONS

1. ALLOCATIONS. Net profits, losses, gains, deductions and credits from operations and financing shall be distributed among the Members in proportion to their respective interest and at such time as shall be determined by the Members.

2. DISTRIBUTIONS. Management may make distributions annually or more frequently if there is excess cash on hand after providing for appropriate expenses and liabilities. Such interim distributions are allocated to each Member according to percentage of membership interest.

ARTICLE V: MANAGEMENT

1. MANAGING MEMBERS. The names and addresses of Managing Members are:

_____

_____

_____

Managing Members shall make decisions regarding the usual affairs of the Company. A majority vote of the membership shall name as many managers as the Membership deem necessary and the membership shall elect one Chief Operating Manager who is responsible for carrying out the decisions of the managers.

2. NUMBER OF MANAGERS. The membership may elect one, but not fewer than one, manager.

3. TERM OF OFFICE. The term of office is not contractual but continues until:

a) A fixed term of office, as designated by the membership, expires.

b) The manager is removed with or without cause, by a majority vote of the membership.

c) The dissociation of such manager.

4. AUTHORITY OF MANAGERS. Only managing members and authorized agents shall have the power to bind the Company. Each managing member is authorized on the Company's behalf to:

a) Purchase, or otherwise acquire, sell, develop, pledge, convey, exchange, lease or otherwise dispose of Company assets wherever located.

b) Initiate, prosecute and defend any proceeding on behalf of the Company.

c) Incur and secure liabilities and obligations on behalf of the Company.

d) Lend, invest or re-invest company assets as security for repayment. Money may be lent to members, employees and agents of the Company.

e) Appoint officers and agents, and hire employees. It is also the province of management to define duties and establish levels of compensation. Management compensation will be determined by majority Membership vote.

f) Execute and deliver all contracts, conveyances, assignments, leases, subleases, franchise and licensing agreements, promissory notes, loans, security agreements or any other kind relating to Company business.

g) Establish pensions, trusts, life insurance, incentive plans or any variation thereof, for the benefit of any or all current or former employees, members and agents of the Company.

h) Make charitable donations in the Company's name.

i) Seek advice from members not part of elected management, although, such advice need not be heeded.

j) Supply, upon the request of any Member, information about the Company or any of its activities including but not limited to, access to company records for the purpose of inspecting and copying company books, records and materials in the possession of management. The Requesting Member shall be responsible for any expenses incurred in the exercise of these rights set forth in this document.

5. STANDARD OF CARE AND EXCULPATION. Any member of management must refrain from engaging in grossly negligent, reckless or intentional misconduct. Any act or omission of a member of management that results in loss or damage to the company or Member, if done in good faith, shall not make the manager liable to the Members.

6. INDEMNIFICATION. The Company shall indemnify its Members, Managers, employees and agents as follows:

a) Every Manager, agent, or employee of the Company shall be indemnified by the Company against all expenses and liabilities, including counsel fees reasonably incurred by him in connection with any proceeding to which he may become involved, by reason of his being or having been a Member of the Company or having served at the request of the Company as a Manager, employee, or agent of the Company or any settlement thereof, whether or not he is a manager, employee or agent at the time such expenses are incurred, except in such cases wherein the Manager, agent or employee is adjudged guilty of willful misfeasance or malfeasance in the performance of his duties; provided that in the event of a settlement the indemnification herein shall apply only when the Managers approve such settlement and reimbursement as being for the best interests of the Company.

b) The Company shall provide to any person who is or was a Member, Manager, employee, or agent of the Company or is or was serving at the request of the Company as Manager, employee, or agent of the Company, the indemnity against expenses of suit, litigation or other proceedings which is specifically permissible under applicable law.

ARTICLE VI: TAX AND ACCOUNTING MATTERS

1. BANK ACCOUNTS. Management shall establish bank accounts, deposit company funds in those accounts and make disbursements from those accounts.

2. ACCOUNTING METHOD. The cash method of accounting shall be the accounting method used to keep records of receipts and disbursements.

3. TMP. A Tax Matter Partner shall be designated by the management of the company as designated by the IRS Code.

4. YEARS. The fiscal and tax years of the Company shall be chosen by management.

5. ACCOUNTANT. An independent accountant shall be selected by management.

ARTICLE VII: MEMBER DISSOCIATION

1. Upon the first occurrence of any of the following events, a person shall cease to be a member of the Company:

a) The bankruptcy of the member.

b) The death or court-ordered adjudication of incapacity of the member.

c) The withdrawal of a member with the consent of a majority vote of the remaining membership.

d) The dissolution and winding up of the non-corporate business member including the termination of a trust.

e) The filing of a Certificate of Dissolution by the corporate member.

f) The complete liquidation of an estate's interest in the LLC.

g) The expulsion of the member with the majority consent of the remaining membership.

h) The expiration of the term specified in Article I, section 6.

2. OPTION TO PURCHASE INTEREST. In the event of dissociation of a Member, the Company shall have the right to purchase the former Member's interest at current fair market value.

ARTICLE VIII: DISPOSITION OF MEMBERSHIP INTERESTS

1. PROHIBITIONS.

    a) No membership interest, be it a sale, assignment, exchange, transfer, mortgage, pledge or grant, shall be disposed of if the disposition would result in the dissolution of the Company without full compliance with all appropriate state and federal laws.

    b) No member may in any way alienate all or part of his membership interest in the Company be it through assignment, conveyance, encumbrance or sale, without the prior written consent of the majority of the remaining members. Such consent may be given, withheld or delayed as the remaining members see fit.

2. PERMISSIONS. A Member may assign his membership interest in the Company subject to the provisions in this article. The assignment of membership interest does not in itself entitle the assignee to participate in the management of the Company nor is the assignee entitled to become a member of the Company. The assignee is not a substitute member but only an assignee of membership interest and as such, is entitled to receive the income and distributions the assigning member would have otherwise received.

3. SUBSTITUTE MEMBERSHIP. Only upon the unanimous consent of the remaining members may an assignee of membership interest become a substitute member and be entitled to all rights associated with the assignor. Upon such admission, the substitute member is subject to all restrictions and liabilities of a Member.

ARTICLE IX: MEETINGS

1. VOTING. All members shall have the right to vote on all of the following:

    a) The dissolution of the Company.

    b) The merger of the Company.

    c) Any transaction involving any potential conflict of interest.

d) An amendment to the Articles of Organization or to the Operating Agreement.

e) The transfer or disposition of all Company assets outside the ordinary course of business.

2. REQUIRED VOTE. Unless a greater vote is required by statute or the Articles of Organization, an affirmative vote of the majority of the membership shall be required.

3. MEETINGS.

a) The manager(s) shall hold an annual meeting at a time and place of their choosing.

b) Special meetings of the membership may be called at any time by the manager(s) or by at least ten (10%) of the membership interest of all members. Written notice of such meeting must be provided at least sixty (60) business days prior and not later than ten (10) days before the date of the meeting. A member may elect to participate in any meeting via telephone.

4. CONSENT. In the absence of an annual or special meeting and in the absence of a vote, any action required to be taken may be permitted with the written consent of the members having not less than the minimum number of votes required to authorize such action at a meeting.

ARTICLE X: DISSOLUTION AND TERMINATION

In the event a dissolution event occurs the remaining membership shall have the option to elect to continue the company as defined by Article I, section 6.

1. MERGER. In the event the election to continue the company following a dissolution event is not obtained, a majority vote of the remaining members may elect to reconstitute the Company through merger with and into another Limited Liability Company pursuant to applicable state law.

2. WINDING UP. If the members do not elect to continue the Company or reconstitute it, the Manager or other person selected by a majority vote of the membership shall wind up the Company.

3. FINAL DISTRIBUTIONS. After all Company assets have been liquidated and all Company debts have been paid, the proceeds of such liquidation shall be distributed to members in accordance with their capital account balance. Liquidation proceeds shall be paid within _____ days of the end of the Company's taxable year or, if later, within _____ days after the date of liquidation.

4. DISSOLUTION. Upon completion of the winding up period, the Manager or other person selected shall file with the Secretary of State the Certificate of Dissolution or its equivalent and any other appropriate documents as required by law.

IN WITNESS WHEREOF, the parties hereto make and execute this Operating Agreement on the dates set below their names, to be effective on the date first above written.

Signed and Agreed this _____ day of _____ , _____ (year).

By

Manager: _____

Member: _____

Member: _____

Member: _____

PLEDGE AGREEMENT OF PERSONAL PROPERTY

FOR VALUE RECEIVED, the undersigned hereby deposits and pledges with
(Pledgee) as collateral security to secure the payment of:
(Describe debt)

The following personal property (collateral) described as:

The parties understand and agree to the following:

1. Pledgee may assign or transfer said debt and said pledged collateral.

2. Pledgee shall have no liability for loss, destruction or casualty to the collateral unless caused by his own negligence.

3. The undersigned shall pay any and all insurance it elects to maintain on the pledged collateral, and any personal property, excise, or other tax or levy.

4. The undersigned warrants that it has good title to the pledged collateral, authority to pledge same, and that it is free from any adverse lien, encumbrance or claim by any third party.

5. In the event of default of payment of the debt or breach of this pledge agreement, the Pledgee or holder shall have full rights to foreclose on the pledged collateral, and exercise its rights as a secured party pursuant to Article 9 of the Uniform Commercial Code; said rights being cumulative with any other rights the Pledgee may have against the undersigned.

In the event of default, Pledgor shall pay all reasonable costs of collection and attorneys' fees.

This pledge agreement shall be binding upon and inure to the benefit of the parties, their successors, assigns and personal representatives.

Signed this   day of   ,   (year).

_____   _____
Pledgee   Pledgor

PLEDGE OF SHARES OF STOCK

FOR VALUE RECEIVED, the undersigned hereby deposits and pledges with
(Pledgee) as collateral security to secure the payment of: (Describe debt)

The following shares of stock, described as (   ) shares of stock of
(Corporation) being Stock Certificate Number(s):

The parties understand and agree to the following:

1. Pledgee may assign or transfer said debt and the stock collateral pledged hereunder.

2. In the event there shall be a stock dividend or further issue of stock in the Corporation to the undersigned, the undersigned shall pledge said shares as additional collateral for the debt.

3. That during the pendency of this pledge agreement, the undersigned shall have full rights to vote said shares and be entitled to all dividend income, and otherwise exercise all rights of the owner of the collateral (except as limited by this agreement).

4. That during the pendency of this agreement, the undersigned shall not issue any proxy or assignment of rights to the pledged shares.

5. The undersigned warrants and represents it has good title to the shares being pledged, they are free from other liens and encumbrances by any third party, and the undersigned has full authority to transfer said shares as collateral security.

6. In the event of default of payment of the debt, or breach of this pledge agreement, the Pledgee or holder shall have full rights to foreclose on the pledged shares, and exercise its rights as a secured party pursuant to Article 9 of the Uniform Commercial Code; said rights being cumulative with any other rights the Pledgee may have against the undersigned.

In the event of default, Pledgor shall pay all reasonable costs of collection and attorneys' fees.

This pledge agreement shall be binding upon and inure to the benefit of the parties, their successors, assigns and personal representatives.

The rights of the Pledgor, upon default, shall be cumulative and not necessarily successive to any other remedy.

Signed this   day of   ,   (year).

_____   _____
Pledgee   Pledgor

199

QUITCLAIM DEED

THIS QUITCLAIM DEED, Executed this   day of
(year),

by first party, Grantor,

whose post office address is

to second party, Grantee,

whose post office address is

WITNESSETH, That the said first party, for good consideration and for the sum of
Dollars ($) paid by the said second
party, the receipt whereof is hereby acknowledged, does hereby remise, release and quitclaim
unto the said second party forever, all the right, title, interest and claim which the said first party
has in and to the following described parcel of land, and improvements and appurtenances thereto in the County of   , State of   to wit:

200

IN WITNESS WHEREOF, The said first party has signed and sealed these presents the day and year first above written. Signed, sealed and delivered in presence of:

_____   _____
Signature of Witness   Signature of First Party

_____   _____
Print name of Witness   Print name of First Party

_____   _____
Signature of Witness   Signature of First Party

_____   _____
Print name of Witness   Print name of First Party

State of   }
County of
On   before me,   '
appeared
personally known to me (or proved to me on the basis of satisfactory evidence) to be the person(s) whose name(s) is/are subscribed to the within instrument and acknowledged to me that he/she/they executed the same in his/her/their authorized capacity(ies), and that by his/her/their signature(s) on the instrument the person(s), or the entity upon behalf of which the person(s) acted, executed the instrument.
WITNESS my hand and official seal.

_____   Affiant _____Known_____Produced ID
Signature of Notary   Type of ID _____
                                                          (Seal)

State of   }
County of
On   before me,   '
appeared
personally known to me (or proved to me on the basis of satisfactory evidence) to be the person(s) whose name(s) is/are subscribed to the within instrument and acknowledged to me that he/she/they executed the same in his/her/their authorized capacity(ies), and that by his/her/their signature(s) on the instrument the person(s), or the entity upon behalf of which the person(s) acted, executed the instrument.
WITNESS my hand and official seal.

_____   Affiant _____Known_____Produced ID
Signature of Notary   Type of ID _____
                                                          (Seal)

                                       _____
                                       Signature of Preparer

                                       _____
                                       Print Name of Preparer

                                       _____
                                       Address of Preparer

ACCOUNT RECORD

Company _____ Account # _____

Address _____

Telephone _____ Fax _____

Name _____ Title _____

Date Account Opened _____ Credit Extended _____

   If delinquent account, original balance due: _____

Date	Invoice #	Amount Paid	Balance Due

Date	Collection History

ACCOUNTS RECEIVABLE AGING

Date:

Account Name	Original Balance	Current Balance	30-60 days	60-90 days	Over 90 days

Totals:

ANNUAL INCOME REPORT

For the Year of _____

Totals for the Month of:	Taxable Sales	Sales Tax	Non-taxable Sales	Total Sales
January				
February				
March				
April				
May				
June				
July				
August				
September				
October				
November				
December				
Totals for the Year:				

BALANCE SHEET

COMPANY NAME: _____

As of _____, _____(year)

ASSETS

Current assets

Cash	$ _____
Petty cash	$ _____
Accounts receivable	$ _____
Inventory	$ _____
Short-term investment	$ _____
Prepaid expenses	$ _____
Long-term investment	$ _____

Fixed assets

Land	$ _____
Buildings	$ _____
Improvements	$ _____
Equipment	$ _____
Furniture	$ _____
Automobile/vehicles	$ _____

Other assets

1.	$ _____
2.	$ _____
3.	$ _____
4.	$ _____
TOTAL ASSETS	$ _____

LIABILITIES

Current Liabilities

Accounts payable	$ _____
Notes payable	$ _____
Interest payable	$ _____
Taxes payable	$ _____
Federal income tax	$ _____
State income tax	$ _____
Self-employment tax	$ _____
Sales tax (SBE)	$ _____
Property tax	$ _____
Payroll accrual	$ _____

Long-term liabilities

Notes payable	$ _____
Total liabilities	$ _____
Net worth (owner equity)	$ _____
Total net worth	$ _____

TOTAL LIABILITIES AND TOTAL NET WORTH	$ _____

(Total assets will always equal total liabilities/total net worth)

INSTRUCTIONS FOR BALANCE SHEET

At the top of the page fill in the legal name of the business, the type of statement and the day, month and year.

Assets

List anything of value that is owned or legally due the business. Total assets include all net values. These are the amounts derived when you subtract depreciation and amortization from the original costs of acquiring the assets.

Current Assets

* Cash — List cash and resources that can be converted into cash within 12 months of the date of the balance sheet (or during one established cycle of operation). Include money on hand and demand deposits in the bank, e.g., checking accounts and regular savings accounts.
* Petty cash — If your business has a fund for small miscellaneous expenditures, include the total here.
* Accounts receivable — The amounts due from customers in payment for merchandise or services.
* Inventory — Includes raw materials on hand, work in progress and all finished goods, either manufactured or purchased for resale.
* Short-term investments — Also called temporary investments or marketable securities, these include interest- or dividend-yielding holdings expected to be converted into cash within a year. List stocks and bonds, certificates of deposit and time-deposit savings accounts at either their cost or market value, whichever is less.
* Prepaid expenses — Goods, benefits or services a business buys or rents in advance. Examples are office supplies, insurance protection and floor space.
* Long-term Investments — Also called long-term assets, these are holdings the business intends to keep for at least a year and that typically yield interest or dividends. Included are stocks, bonds and savings accounts earmarked for special purposes.

Fixed Assets

Also called plant and equipment. Includes all resources a business owns or acquires for use in operations and not intended for resale. Fixed assets may be leased. Depending on the leasing arrangements, both the value and the liability of the leased property may need to be listed on the balance sheet.

* Land (list original purchase price)
* Buildings
* Improvements
* Equipment
* Furniture
* Automobile/vehicles

Liabilities

Current Liabilities

List all debts, monetary obligations and claims payable within 12 months or within one cycle of operation. Typically they include the following:

* Accounts payable — Amounts owed to suppliers for goods and services purchased in connection with business operations.
* Notes payable — The balance of principal due to pay off short-term debt for borrowed funds. Also includes the current amount due of total balance on notes whose terms exceed 12 months.
* Interest payable — Any accrued fees due for use of both short- and long-term borrowed capital and credit extended to the business.
* Taxes payable — Amounts estimated by an accountant to have been incurred during the accounting period.
* Payroll accrual — Salaries and wages currently owed.

Long-term Liabilities

* Notes payable — List notes, contract payments or mortgage payments due over a period exceeding 12 months or one cycle of operation. They are listed by outstanding balance less the current amount due.
* Net worth — Also called owner's equity, net worth is the claim of the owner(s) on the assets of the business. In a proprietorship or partnership, equity is each owner's original investment plus any earnings after withdrawals.

Total Liabilities and Net Worth

The sum of these two amounts must always match that for total assets.

EMPLOYEE PAYROLL RECORD

Name _____

Address _____

Social Security # _____

Pay Rate _____

Direct Deposit Auth. # _____

Payment Date	Check #	Pay Period	HOURS Reg.	HOURS Over.	Gross	F.I.T.	Social Security	Medicare	State Income	Other Withhold.	Other	Net Pay

INVENTORY RECORD

Item	Supplier	Date Ordered	Quantity Ordered	Date Rec'd	Quantity Rec'd	Quantity Sold	Balance In Stock

MONTHLY CASH FLOW PROJECTION–PRE-START-UP

Name of Business_____ Owner _____ Type of Business_____
Prepared by _____ Date prepared_____ Year _____ Month _____

1. Cash on hand (beginning of month)   _____
2. Cash receipts
   (a) Cash sales   _____
   (b) Collections from credit accounts   _____
   (c) Loan or other cash injections (specify) _____
3. Total cash receipts (2a+2b+2c=3)   _____
4. Total cash available (before cash out) (1+3) _____
5. Cash paid out
   (a) purchases (merchandise)   _____
   (b) Gross wages (excludes withdrawals)   _____
   (c) Payroll expenses (taxes, etc.)   _____
   (d) Outside services   _____
   (e) Supplies (office and operating)   _____
   (f) Repairs and maintenance   _____
   (g) Advertising   _____
   (h) Car, delivery and travel   _____
   (i) Accounting and legal   _____
   (j) Rent   _____
   (k) Telephone   _____
   (l) Utilities   _____
   (m) Insurance   _____
   (n) Taxes (real estate, etc.)   _____
   (o) Interest   _____
   (p) Other expenses (specify)   _____

   (q) Miscellaneous   _____
   (r) Subtotal   _____
   (s) Loan principal payment   _____
   (t) Capital purchases (specify)   _____
   (u) Other start-up costs   _____
   (v) Reserve and/or escrow (specify)   _____
   (w) Owner's withdrawal   _____
6. Total cash paid out (5a through 5w)   _____
7. Cash position (end of month) (4 minus 6) _____
Essential operating data (non-cash flow information)
   A. Sales volume (dollars)   _____
   B. Accounts receivable (end on month)   _____
   C. Bad debt (end of month)   _____
   D. Inventory on hand (end of month)   _____
   E. Accounts payable (end of month)   _____

210

MONTHLY CASH FLOW PROJECTION–FIRST MONTH

Name of Business_____ Owner _____ Type of Business_____
Prepared by _____ Date prepared_____ Year _____ Month _____

1. Cash on hand (beginning of month) _____
2. Cash receipts
   (a) Cash sales _____
   (b) Collections from credit accounts _____
   (c) Loan or other cash injections (specify) _____
3. Total cash receipts (2a+2b+2c=3) _____
4. Total cash available (before cash out) (1+3) _____
5. Cash paid out
   (a) purchases (merchandise) _____
   (b) Gross wages (excludes withdrawals) _____
   (c) Payroll expenses (taxes, etc.) _____
   (d) Outside services _____
   (e) Supplies (office and operating) _____
   (f) Repairs and maintenance _____
   (g) Advertising _____
   (h) Car, delivery and travel _____
   (i) Accounting and legal _____
   (j) Rent _____
   (k) Telephone _____
   (l) Utilities _____
   (m) Insurance _____
   (n) Taxes (real estate, etc.) _____
   (o) Interest _____
   (p) Other expenses (specify) _____
   _____
   (q) Miscellaneous _____
   (r) Subtotal _____
   (s) Loan principal payment _____
   (t) Capital purchases (specify) _____
   (u) Reserve and/or escrow (specify) _____
   (v) Owner's withdrawal _____
6. Total cash paid out (5a through 5w) _____
7. Cash position (end of month) (4 minus 6) _____
Essential operating data (non-cash flow information)
   A. Sales volume (dollars) _____
   B. Accounts receivable (end on month) _____
   C. Bad debt (end of month) _____
   D. Inventory on hand (end of month) _____
   E. Accounts payable (end of month) _____

211

MONTHLY CASH FLOW PROJECTION—SECOND MONTH

Name of Business_____ Owner _____ Type of Business_____

Prepared by _____ Date prepared_____ Year _____ Month _____

1. Cash on hand (beginning of month) _____
2. Cash receipts
   (a) Cash sales _____
   (b) Collections from credit accounts _____
   (c) Loan or other cash injections (specify) _____
3. Total cash receipts (2a+2b+2c=3) _____
4. Total cash available (before cash out) (1+3) _____
5. Cash paid out
   (a) purchases (merchandise) _____
   (b) Gross wages (excludes withdrawals) _____
   (c) Payroll expenses (taxes, etc.) _____
   (d) Outside services _____
   (e) Supplies (office and operating) _____
   (f) Repairs and maintenance _____
   (g) Advertising _____
   (h) Car, delivery and travel _____
   (i) Accounting and legal _____
   (j) Rent _____
   (k) Telephone _____
   (l) Utilities _____
   (m) Insurance _____
   (n) Taxes (real estate, etc.) _____
   (o) Interest _____
   (p) Other expenses (specify) _____

   (q) Miscellaneous _____
   (r) Subtotal _____
   (s) Loan principal payment _____
   (t) Capital purchases (specify) _____
   (u) Reserve and/or escrow (specify) _____
   (v) Owner's withdrawal _____
6. Total cash paid out (5a through 5w) _____
7. Cash position (end of month) (4 minus 6) _____

Essential operating data (non-cash flow information)
   A. Sales volume (dollars) _____
   B. Accounts receivable (end on month) _____
   C. Bad debt (end of month) _____
   D. Inventory on hand (end of month) _____
   E. Accounts payable (end of month) _____

212

MONTHLY CASH FLOW PROJECTION–THIRD MONTH

Name of Business_____ Owner _____ Type of Business_____
Prepared by _____ Date prepared_____ Year _____ Month _____

1. Cash on hand (beginning of month)   _____
2. Cash receipts
    (a) Cash sales   _____
    (b) Collections from credit accounts   _____
    (c) Loan or other cash injections (specify)   _____
3. Total cash receipts (2a+2b+2c=3)   _____
4. Total cash available (before cash out) (1+3)   _____
5. Cash paid out
    (a) purchases (merchandise)   _____
    (b) Gross wages (excludes withdrawals)   _____
    (c) Payroll expenses (taxes, etc.)   _____
    (d) Outside services   _____
    (e) Supplies (office and operating)   _____
    (f) Repairs and maintenance   _____
    (g) Advertising   _____
    (h) Car, delivery and travel   _____
    (i) Accounting and legal   _____
    (j) Rent   _____
    (k) Telephone   _____
    (l) Utilities   _____
    (m) Insurance   _____
    (n) Taxes (real estate, etc.)   _____
    (o) Interest   _____
    (p) Other expenses (specify)   _____
                                                            _____
    (q) Miscellaneous   _____
    (r) Subtotal   _____
    (s) Loan principal payment   _____
    (t) Capital purchases (specify)   _____
    (u) Reserve and/or escrow (specify)   _____
    (v) Owner's withdrawal   _____
6. Total cash paid out (5a through 5w)   _____
7. Cash position (end of month) (4 minus 6)   _____
Essential operating data (non-cash flow information)
    A. Sales volume (dollars)   _____
    B. Accounts receivable (end on month)   _____
    C. Bad debt (end of month)   _____
    D. Inventory on hand (end of month)   _____
    E. Accounts payable (end of month)   _____

213

MONTHLY CASH FLOW PROJECTION–FOURTH MONTH

Name of Business_____ Owner _____ Type of Business_____

Prepared by _____ Date prepared_____ Year _____ Month _____

1. Cash on hand (beginning of month) _____
2. Cash receipts
   (a) Cash sales _____
   (b) Collections from credit accounts _____
   (c) Loan or other cash injections (specify) _____
3. Total cash receipts (2a+2b+2c=3) _____
4. Total cash available (before cash out) (1+3) _____
5. Cash paid out
   (a) purchases (merchandise) _____
   (b) Gross wages (excludes withdrawals) _____
   (c) Payroll expenses (taxes, etc.) _____
   (d) Outside services _____
   (e) Supplies (office and operating) _____
   (f) Repairs and maintenance _____
   (g) Advertising _____
   (h) Car, delivery and travel _____
   (i) Accounting and legal _____
   (j) Rent _____
   (k) Telephone _____
   (l) Utilities _____
   (m) Insurance _____
   (n) Taxes (real estate, etc.) _____
   (o) Interest _____
   (p) Other expenses (specify) _____
   _____
   (q) Miscellaneous _____
   (r) Subtotal _____
   (s) Loan principal payment _____
   (t) Capital purchases (specify) _____
   (u) Reserve and/or escrow (specify) _____
   (v) Owner's withdrawal _____
6. Total cash paid out (5a through 5w) _____
7. Cash position (end of month) (4 minus 6) _____
Essential operating data (non-cash flow information)
   A. Sales volume (dollars) _____
   B. Accounts receivable (end on month) _____
   C. Bad debt (end of month) _____
   D. Inventory on hand (end of month) _____
   E. Accounts payable (end of month) _____

214

MONTHLY CASH FLOW PROJECTION–FIFTH MONTH

Name of Business_____ Owner _____ Type of Business_____
Prepared by _____ Date prepared_____ Year _____ Month _____

1. Cash on hand (beginning of month)   _____
2. Cash receipts
   (a) Cash sales   _____
   (b) Collections from credit accounts   _____
   (c) Loan or other cash injections (specify)   _____
3. Total cash receipts (2a+2b+2c=3)   _____
4. Total cash available (before cash out) (1+3)   _____
5. Cash paid out
   (a) purchases (merchandise)   _____
   (b) Gross wages (excludes withdrawals)   _____
   (c) Payroll expenses (taxes, etc.)   _____
   (d) Outside services   _____
   (e) Supplies (office and operating)   _____
   (f) Repairs and maintenance   _____
   (g) Advertising   _____
   (h) Car, delivery and travel   _____
   (i) Accounting and legal   _____
   (j) Rent   _____
   (k) Telephone   _____
   (l) Utilities   _____
   (m) Insurance   _____
   (n) Taxes (real estate, etc.)   _____
   (o) Interest   _____
   (p) Other expenses (specify)   _____
   _____
   (q) Miscellaneous   _____
   (r) Subtotal   _____
   (s) Loan principal payment   _____
   (t) Capital purchases (specify)   _____
   (u) Reserve and/or escrow (specify)   _____
   (v) Owner's withdrawal   _____
6. Total cash paid out (5a through 5w)   _____
7. Cash position (end of month) (4 minus 6)   _____
Essential operating data (non-cash flow information)
   A. Sales volume (dollars)   _____
   B. Accounts receivable (end on month)   _____
   C. Bad debt (end of month)   _____
   D. Inventory on hand (end of month)   _____
   E. Accounts payable (end of month)   _____

215

MONTHLY CASH FLOW PROJECTION–SIXTH MONTH

Name of Business_____ Owner _____ Type of Business_____
Prepared by _____ Date prepared_____ Year _____ Month _____

TOTALS Months 1-6

1. Cash on hand (beginning of month) _____ _____
2. Cash receipts
   (a) Cash sales _____ _____
   (b) Collections from credit accounts _____ _____
   (c) Loan or other cash injections (specify) _____ _____
3. Total cash receipts (2a+2b+2c=3) _____ _____
4. Total cash available (before cash out) (1+3) _____ _____
5. Cash paid out
   (a) purchases (merchandise) _____ _____
   (b) Gross wages (excludes withdrawals) _____ _____
   (c) Payroll expenses (taxes, etc.) _____ _____
   (d) Outside services _____ _____
   (e) Supplies (office and operating) _____ _____
   (f) Repairs and maintenance _____ _____
   (g) Advertising _____ _____
   (h) Car, delivery and travel _____ _____
   (i) Accounting and legal _____ _____
   (j) Rent _____ _____
   (k) Telephone _____ _____
   (l) Utilities _____ _____
   (m) Insurance _____ _____
   (n) Taxes (real estate, etc.) _____ _____
   (o) Interest _____ _____
   (p) Other expenses (specify) _____ _____

   (q) Miscellaneous _____ _____
   (r) Subtotal _____ _____
   (s) Loan principal payment _____ _____
   (t) Capital purchases (specify) _____ _____
   (u) Reserve and/or escrow (specify) _____ _____
   (v) Owner's withdrawal _____ _____
6. Total cash paid out (5a through 5w) _____ _____
7. Cash position (end of month) (4 minus 6) _____ _____
Essential operating data (non-cash flow information)
   A. Sales volume (dollars) _____ _____
   B. Accounts receivable (end on month) _____ _____
   C. Bad debt (end of month) _____ _____
   D. Inventory on hand (end of month) _____ _____
   E. Accounts payable (end of month) _____ _____

216

INSTRUCTIONS FOR MONTHLY CASH FLOW PROJECTION

1. Cash on hand (beginning of month)

Cash on hand same as (7), Cash position, previous month

2. Cash receipts

(a) Cash sales— All cash sales. Omit credit sales unless cash is actually received

(b) Gross wages (including withdrawals)—Amount to be expected from all accounts.

(c) Loan or other cash injection—Indicate here all cash injections not shown in 2(a) or 2(b) above.

3. Total cash receipts (2a+2b+2c=3)

4. Total cash available (before cash paid out)(1+3)

5. Cash paid out

(a) Purchases (merchandise)—Merchandise for resale or for use in product (paid for in current month).

(b) Gross wages (including withdrawals)—Base pay plus overtime (if any)

(c) Payroll expenses (taxes, etc.)— Include paid vacations, paid sick leave, health insurance, unemployment insurance (this might be 10 to 45% of 5(b))

(d) Outside services—This could include outside labor and/or material for specialized or overflow work, including subcontracting

(e) Supplies (office and operating)—Items purchased for use in the business (not for resale)

(f) Repairs and maintenance— Include periodic large expenditures such as painting or decorating

(g) Advertising—This amount should be adequate to maintain sales volume

(h) Car, delivery and travel—If personal car is used, charge in this column, include parking

(i) Accounting and legal—Outside services, including, for example, bookkeeping

(j) Rent— Real estate only (See 5(p) for other rentals)

(k) Telephone

(l) Utilities—Water, heat, light and/or power

(m) Insurance— Coverage on business property and products (fire, liability); also worker's compensation, fidelity, etc. Exclude executive life (include in 5(w))

(n) Taxes (real estate, etc.)— Plus inventory tax, sales tax, excise tax, if applicable

(o) Interest—Remember to add interest on loan as it is injected (See 2(c) above)

(p) Other expenses (specify each)

_____

_____

Unexpected expenditures may be included here as a safety factor

_____

Equipment expenses during the month should be included here (non-capital equipment)

_____

When equipment is rented or leased, record payments here

_____

_____

(q) Miscellaneous (unspecified)—Small expenditures for which separate accounts would be practical

(r) Subtotal—This subtotal indicates cash out for operating costs

(s) Loan principal payment—Include payment on all loans, including vehicle and equipment purchases on time payment

(t) Capital purchases (specify)—Nonexpensed (depreciable) expenditures such as equipment, building purchases on time payment

(u) Other start-up costs—Expenses incurred prior to first month projection and paid for after start-up

(v) Reserve and/or escrow (specify)— Example: insurance, tax or equipment escrow to reduce impact of large periodic payments

(w) Owner's withdrawals— Should include payment for such things as owner's income tax, social security, health insurance, executive life insurance premiums, etc.

6. Total cash paid out (5a through 5w)

7. Cash position (end of month)
(4 minus 6)— Enter this amount in (1) Cash on hand following month—

Essential operating data (non-cash flow information)

This is basic information necessary for proper planning and for proper cash flow projection. Also with this data, the cash flow can be evolved and shown in the above form.

A. **Sales volume (dollars)**—This is a very important figure and should be estimated carefully, taking into account size of facility and employee output as well as realistically anticipated sales (actual sales, not orders received).

B. **Accounts receivable (end of month)**— Previous unpaid credit sales plus current month's credit sales, less amounts received current month (deduct "C" below)

C. **Bad debt (end of month)**— Bad debts should be subtracted from (B) in the month anticipated

D. **Inventory on hand (end of month)**— Last month's inventory plus merchandise received and/or manufactured current month minus amount sold current month

E. **Accounts payable (end of month)**— Previous month's payable plus current month's payable minus amount paid during month.

F. **Depreciation**—Established by your accountant, or value of all your equipment divided by useful life (in months) as allowed by Internal Revenue Service.

MONTHLY EXPENSE REPORT

For the Month of _____

Date	Check #	Payee	Inventory	Begin Supplies	Outside Contractors	Payroll	Advertising	Rent	Utilities	Taxes and Licenses	Misc.	Total

MONTHLY INCOME REPORT

For the Month of _____

Date	Sales Period	Taxable Sales	Sales Tax	Non-taxable Sales	Total Sales

Totals for the Month:

PETTY CASH RECORD

For the Period:_____ Opening Balance:_____ Date Posted:_____

Date	Activity	Department	Amount	Balance
_____	_____	_____	_____	_____
_____	_____	_____	_____	_____
_____	_____	_____	_____	_____
_____	_____	_____	_____	_____
_____	_____	_____	_____	_____
_____	_____	_____	_____	_____
_____	_____	_____	_____	_____
_____	_____	_____	_____	_____
_____	_____	_____	_____	_____
_____	_____	_____	_____	_____
_____	_____	_____	_____	_____
_____	_____	_____	_____	_____
_____	_____	_____	_____	_____
_____	_____	_____	_____	_____
_____	_____	_____	_____	_____
_____	_____	_____	_____	_____

TOTAL TO BE
REIMBURSED: _____

PROJECTED BUDGET

For the month of _____

	Estimate	Actual	Difference	%
Employees				
payroll	_____	_____	_____	_____
insurance	_____	_____	_____	_____
benefits	_____	_____	_____	_____
dues/subscriptions	_____	_____	_____	_____
Building				
rent/mortgage	_____	_____	_____	_____
insurance	_____	_____	_____	_____
telephone	_____	_____	_____	_____
utilities	_____	_____	_____	_____
maintenance/repairs	_____	_____	_____	_____
Office				
supplies	_____	_____	_____	_____
equipment	_____	_____	_____	_____
inventory	_____	_____	_____	_____
postage	_____	_____	_____	_____
shipping/storage	_____	_____	_____	_____
sales expenses	_____	_____	_____	_____
advertising	_____	_____	_____	_____
Legal & accounting				
attorney	_____	_____	_____	_____
accountant	_____	_____	_____	_____
taxes	_____	_____	_____	_____
auditing	_____	_____	_____	_____
interest	_____	_____	_____	_____
bad debts	_____	_____	_____	_____
insurance	_____	_____	_____	_____
other	_____	_____	_____	_____
TOTALS:	_____	_____	_____	_____

COLLECTION REPORT

Date:

Customer Name:_____ Acct. No.:_____

Street: _____

City: _____ State: _____ Zip: _____

Phone: _____ Contact: _____

Period ending: _____

Account Status:

Current Balance $ _____

30 days $ _____

60 days $ _____

Over 90 Days $ _____

Agreement for payments?

Compliance?

Recommended Action:

_____   Continue credit

_____   Stop credit and negotiate payment plan

_____   Stop credit and collect

_____   Other

By: _____

CREDIT CHANGE NOTICE

Date:

To: Credit Department

Sales Personnel

Customer File

New credit terms/limits are effective immediately for the following account:

Customer Name: _____

Address: _____

City: _____State: _____Zip: _____

Account No.:_____ New Account: _____

Current Account: _____

Renewed Account: _____

Sales Representative _____

New credit limit: $

Changed from prior limit of: $

Other terms:

Agreement on prior balance:

By: _____

CREDIT/COLLECTION ANALYSIS

Company: _____ Date: _____

AGED BALANCE COMPARISONS

As of _____ , (year).   As of _____ , (year).

AMOUNT IN $

$ _____	Current	$ _____
$ _____	30-60 days	$ _____
$ _____	60-90 days	$ _____
$ _____	Over 90 days	$ _____
_____		_____
$ _____	**Total Accounts Receivable:**	$ _____

AMOUNT IN %

( )%	Current	( )%
( )%	30-60 days	( )%
( )%	60-90 days	( )%
( )%	Over 90 days	( )%

Amounts due on notes or repayment agreement, and not included above:

$_____ $_____
This Period   Prior Period

Charged off as uncollectible:

$_____ $_____
This Period   Prior Period

Average collection period/days:

$_____
 This Period

$_____
 Prior Period

Average charge sales/day:

$_____
 This Period

$_____
 Prior Period

Credit losses as a percentage of sales:

$_____
 This Period

$_____
 Prior Period

Number of open accounts:

$_____
 This Period

$_____
 Prior Period

Percentage of charge sales to total sales:

_____%
This Period

_____%
Prior Period

Receivable turnover ratio:

_____%
This Period

_____%
Prior Period

Daily sales outstanding:

_____days
This Period

_____days
Prior Period

Credit department expense:

_____%
This Period

_____%
Prior Period

Comments:

CREDIT INFORMATION CHECKLIST

Customer: _____

Address: _____

City: _____ State: _____ Zip: _____

Telephone No.: _____ Contact: _____

Date of Order or Credit Request: _____

Sales Representative: _____

	Date Requested	Date Received	Date Approved
Credit Application	_____	_____	_____
Financial Statements	_____	_____	_____
Inspection Report	_____	_____	_____
Bank Reference	_____	_____	_____
Trade References:			
_____	_____	_____	_____
_____	_____	_____	_____
_____	_____	_____	_____
Sales Report	_____	_____	_____
D & B Report	_____	_____	_____
Other Credit Reports:			
_____	_____	_____	_____
_____	_____	_____	_____
_____	_____	_____	_____
Guarantor's Financials	_____	_____	_____
Lien/Security Check	_____	_____	_____
Insurance Verification	_____	_____	_____
Other:			
_____	_____	_____	_____

CREDIT POLICY

1. Procedures for Approving Credit:

2. Standard Credit Terms:

3. Account Review Procedures:

4. Collection Procedures:

Exceptions to this Credit Policy <u>must</u> be approved by the credit manager.

CUSTOMER CREDIT ANALYSIS

Customer:_____ Date:_____

Address:_____ Phone:_____

City:_____ State:_____ Zip: _____

Account No.: _____

D & B Rating:_____

Other Credit Ratings:_____

_____

	Excellent	Good	Fair	Poor
Bank Reference:	____	____	____	____
_____				
Credit Reference:	____	____	____	____
_____				
Credit Reference:	____	____	____	____
_____				
Credit Reference:	____	____	____	____
_____				
Credit Report:	____	____	____	____
_____				
Credit Report:	____	____	____	____
_____				
Other:	____	____	____	____

FINANCIAL ANALYSIS SUMMARY

	Excellent	Good	Fair	Poor
Balance Sheet:	____	____	____	____
Income Statement:	____	____	____	____

SUMMARY:

Credit Recommended:_____

Credit Approved: _____

NEW ACCOUNT CREDIT APPROVAL

Customer:_____

Address:_____ City:_____ State:_____ Zip:_____

Phone:_____ Contact:_____

Sales Representative:_____ Date:_____

Credit Line: $ _____

Shipment Terms:

Payment Terms:

Initial Order Terms:

Other Terms:

Credit Review By:

Approved By: _____

PROMISSORY NOTE

$ _____   Dated: _____ , _____ (year)

Principal Amount   State of _____

       FOR VALUE RECEIVED, the undersigned hereby jointly and severally promise to pay to the order of _____ , the sum of _____ Dollars ($ _____), together with interest thereon at the rate of _____ % per annum on the unpaid balance. Said sum shall be paid in the manner following:

       All payments shall be first applied to interest and the balance to principal. This note may be prepaid, at any time, in whole or in part, without penalty. All prepayments shall be applied in reverse order of maturity.

       This note shall at the option of any holder hereof be immediately due and payable upon the failure to make any payment due hereunder within _____ days of its due date.

       In the event this note shall be in default, and placed with an attorney for collection, then the undersigned agree to pay all reasonable attorney fees and costs of collection. Payments not made within five (5) days of due date shall be subject to a late charge of _____ % of said payment. All payments hereunder shall be made to such address as may from time to time be designated by any holder hereof.

       The undersigned and all other parties to this note, whether as endorsers, guarantors or sureties, agree to remain fully bound hereunder until this note shall be fully paid and waive demand, presentment and protest and all notices thereto and further agree to remain bound, notwithstanding any extension, renewal, modification, waiver, or other indulgence by any holder or upon the discharge or release of any obligor hereunder or to this note, or upon the exchange, substitution, or release of any collateral granted as security for this note. No modification or indulgence by any holder hereof shall be binding unless in writing; and any indulgence on any one occasion shall not be an indulgence for any other or future occasion. Any modification or change of terms, hereunder granted by any holder hereof, shall be valid and binding upon each of the undersigned, notwithstanding the acknowledgment of any of the undersigned, and each of the undersigned does hereby irrevocably grant to each of the others a power of attorney to enter into any such modification on their behalf. The rights of any holder hereof shall be cumulative and not necessarily successive. This note shall take effect as a sealed instrument and shall be construed, governed and enforced in accordance with the laws of the State first appearing at the head of this note. The undersigned hereby execute this note as principals and not as sureties.

Signed in the presence of:

_____   _____

Witness   Borrower

_____   _____

Witness   Borrower

GUARANTY

       We the undersigned jointly and severally guaranty the prompt and punctual payment of all moneys due under the aforesaid note and agree to remain bound until fully paid.

In the presence of:

_____   _____

Witness   Guarantor

_____   _____

Witness   Guarantor

REQUEST FOR BANK CREDIT REFERENCE

Date:

To:

Re:

The above-mentioned customer has referred us to you as a banking reference. In order for us to grant credit to the customer, we would appreciate your providing us the following information:

1.　How long has the customer maintained an account with you?

2.　What is the average account balance?

3.　Does the customer routinely have over drafts?

4.　Is the customer a borrowing or non-borrowing account?

5.　If the customer borrows, please inform as to:

Balance on secured loans　　$ _____

Balance on unsecured loans　$ _____

Terms of repayment: _____

Is repayment satisfactory:_____

We would greatly appreciate any additional comments or information you can provide concerning this account. We would also appreciate future information on substantial changes in the customer's financial situation or banking relations with you.

Of course, all information furnished shall be held in strict confidence. Thank you for providing the requested information, and if we may ever be of assistance, please let us know.

Very truly,

_____

REQUEST FOR PREPAYMENT

Date:

To:

Thank you for your order dated   ,   (year). We regret to inform you that we can not ship the products ordered on credit or on C.O.D. terms for the following reason:

However, we would be pleased to promptly process and ship your order upon prepayment of the order in the amount of $.

We look forward to your payment so that we may expedite your order.

Again, we thank you for your cooperation and patronage.

Very truly,

_____

CONFIDENTIALITY AGREEMENT

The nature of services provided by
(Company) requires information to be handled in a private, confidential manner.

Information about our business or our employees or clients will only be released to people or agencies outside the company with our written consent. Following legal or regulatory guidelines provide the only exceptions to this policy. All reports, memoranda, notes, or other documents will remain part of the company's confidential records.

The names, addresses, phone numbers or salaries of our employees will only be released to people authorized by the nature of their duties to receive such information and only with the consent of management or the employee.

The undersigned employee agrees to abide by this confidentiality agreement.

_____   _____
Employee   Date

_____   _____
Witness   Date

EMPLOYEE AGREEMENT
AND HANDBOOK ACKNOWLEDGEMENT

This employee handbook and the personnel policy manual highlight the company policies, procedures, and benefits. In all instances the official benefit plan texts, trust agreements and master contracts are the governing documents. Your employee handbook is not to be interpreted as a legal document or an employment contract. Employment with the company is at the sole discretion of the company and may be terminated with or without cause at any time and for any reason. Nothing in this handbook or in the personnel policy manual constitutes an express or implied contract or assurance of continued employment, or implies that just cause is required for termination.

Understood and agreed:

_____

Employee

_____

Date

EMPLOYEE WELCOME LETTER

Date:

To:

Dear   :

    At   m. ,   ,   (year), you are to report for
work at the personnel office of
We hope you are looking forward to this event as enthusiastically as we are.

    You are now a member of a fine group of people operating as a team with the
common objective of providing

    We are very happy that you have chosen us for your career. We look forward to
seeing you on your starting day.

                              Very truly yours,

                           _____

EMPLOYMENT APPLICATION
(please print)

Full Name: _____

Address: _____

City: _____ State: _____ Zip: _____

Phone: _____ Social Security No: _____

Position Applied For: _____

Are you a citizen of the United States? ☐ Yes ☐ No

If not, do you have work papers? _____

Do you voluntarily identify yourself as a veteran for reporting purposes? ☐ Yes ☐ No

EDUCATION
(name and location of school)

High School: _____

Did you graduate? _____ Degree: _____

Bus./Trade: _____

Did you graduate? _____ Degree: _____

Col./Univ.: _____

Did you graduate? _____ Degree: _____

Grad./Prof.: _____

Did you graduate? _____ Degree: _____

PREVIOUS EMPLOYMENT
(begin with most recent position)

Most recent

Firm: _____ Address: _____

Supervisor: _____ Nature of Business: _____

Dates of Employment: _____ Position(s) Held: _____

Ending Salary: _____ Reason for Leaving: _____

Previous Employer

Firm: _____ Address: _____

Supervisor: _____ Nature of Business: _____

Dates of Employment: _____ Position(s) Held: _____

Ending Salary: _____ Reason for Leaving: _____

Previous Employer

Firm: _____ Address: _____

Supervisor: _____ Nature of Business: _____

Dates of employment: _____ Position(s) Held: _____

Ending Salary: _____ Reason for Leaving: _____

REFERENCES

Please furnish the names and addresses of two people to whom you are not related and by whom you have not been employed.

Name: _____

Address: _____

Name: _____

Address: _____

Who referred you to us? (person or agency): _____

_____

Summarize your special skills or qualifications:

_____

_____

_____

I certify that my answers are true and complete to the best of my knowledge.

I authorize you to make such investigations and inquiries of my personal, employment, educational, financial, or medical history and other related matters as may be necessary for an employment decision. I hereby release employers, schools, or persons from all liability in responding to inquiries in connection with my application.

In the event I am employed, I understand that false or misleading information given in my application or interview(s) may result in discharge.

Signature of Applicant: _____ Date: _____

For Department Use Only

Action: _____

_____

_____

_____

INDEPENDENT CONTRACTOR'S AGREEMENT

Contract made on this   day of   ,
, between: , herein referred to as Owner,
doing business at   , City of
                              State of   , and
                                                   , herein referred to as
Contractor, doing business at   , City of
                              State of

.

RECITALS

1. Owner operates a   business at the address set forth above and desires to have the following services performed at Owner's place of business:

2. Contractor agrees to perform these services for Owner under the terms and
conditions set forth in this contract.

In consideration of the mutual promises contained herein, it is agreed:

A. Description of Work: The Contractor shall perform all services generally related to Contractor's usual line of business, including, but not limited to, the following:

239

B. Payment: Owner will pay Contractor the sum of
Dollars ($) for the
work performed under this contract, under the following schedule:

C. Relationship of Parties: This contract creates an independent contractor-employer relationship. Owner is interested only in the results to be achieved. Contractor is solely responsible for the conduct and control of the work. Contractor is not an agent or employee of Owner for any purpose. Employees of Contractor are not entitled to any benefits that Owner provides Owner's employees. This is not an exclusive agreement. Both parties are free to contract with other parties for similar services.

D. Liability: Contractor assumes all risk connected with work to be performed. Contractor also accepts all responsibility for the condition of tools and equipment used in the performance of this contract and will carry for the duration of this contract public liability insurance in an amount acceptable to Owner. Contractor agrees to indemnify Owner for any and all liability or loss arising from the performance of this contract.

E. Duration: Either party may cancel this contract with days' written notice; otherwise, the contract shall remain in force for a term of from date hereof.

In witness whereof, the parties have executed this agreement in the City of
, State of , the
day and year first above written.

_____   _____
(Signature of Owner)   (Signature of Contractor)

JOB APPLICANT RATING

Applicant:_____

Position: _____

Department: _____

Use the following scale to rate applicant's qualifications:

5) Excellent	2) Below Average
4) Above Average	1) Unacceptable
3) Fully qualified	0) Unobserved

Education _____

Experience _____

Attention to Detail _____

Cooperation _____

Initiative _____

Integrity _____

Interpersonal Skills _____

Learning Ability _____

Stress Tolerance _____

Verbal Communication _____

Overall:

_____Exceptional   _____Strong   _____Acceptable

_____Weak   _____ Totally unacceptable

Recommendation:

_____Hire

_____Reject

_____Other _____

Signed:

_____   _____
Interviewer   Date

JOB DESCRIPTION

Position:

Basic Function:

Scope of work:

Principal Accountabilities:

Principal Interactions:

Knowledge/Education Requirements:

Authority Level:

Reports to:

NOTICE OF AVAILABLE POSITION

Starting Date: _____ Date Posted: _____

Position: _____

Description Of Duties:

Qualifications Required:

Salary:

Contact:

We are an Affirmative Action/Equal Opportunity Employer

AGREEMENT WITH SALES REPRESENTATIVE

Agreement dated   ,   , between
(the Company) and
(the Sales Representative).

THE SALES REPRESENTATIVE AGREES TO:

1. Represent and sell the Company's line described as:

within the geographic area of:

2. State accurately company policies to all potential customers.

3. Promptly submit all orders to the sales manager.

4. Notify the sales manager of all problems of concern to the Company relating to customers within the sales territory.

5. Inform the sales manager if the Sales Representative is representing, or plans to represent, any other business firm. In no event may the Sales Representative represent a competitive product line.

6. Telephone the sales manager at least   to discuss sales activity in the territory.

7. Give one month's notice in writing to the sales manager if the Sales Representative wishes to terminate this agreement.

8. Promptly return all materials provided by the Company to the Sales Representative, if either party terminates this agreement.

THE COMPANY AGREES:

1. To pay the following commissions to the Sales Representative:

2. To negotiate in advance of sale the commission percentage to be paid on all orders where the Sales Representative requests a quantity discount or other trade concession be granted to a customer.

3. Refunds to customers or merchandise returned by the customer where a commission has already been paid to the Sales Representative, shall be deducted from future commissions to be paid to the Sales Representative.

4. For purposes of sales credit, a sale is defined as an order from a customer that was initiated by the personal action of the Sales Representative and delivered by the Sales Representative to the sales department of the Company.

5. Company shall provide the Sales Representative with business cards, brochures, catalogs, and any product samples required for demonstration purposes.

6. Company shall set minimum monthly quotas after consultation with the Sales Representative.

7. Company shall give one month's notice, in writing, if the Company wishes to terminate this agreement.

8. To pay all commissions owed to the Sales Representative for a period of _____ months after this agreement is terminated by either party. Nothing in this agreement grants an exclusive sales territory to the Sales Representative. The Company shall continue to send direct mail advertising and have telemarketers solicit within the assigned territory of the Sales Representative.

_____   _____
Company   Sales Representative

_____
By

_____   _____
Date   Date

Glossary of useful terms

A-B

Accrual method
A financial record-keeping system that credits income when earned or due and expenses when incurred, regardless of actual cash receipts or disbursements.

Adjusted basis
Original cost or value adjusted by additions and depreciation.

Affirmative action
Government guidelines requiring an employer to hire minority employees in order to remedy past employment discrimination.

Arbitration
A method for settling a dispute by a quasi-judicial procedure as provided by law or agreement; arbitrator's judgment is usually binding on all parties.

Articles of Organization
A document filed with the Secretary of State that creates a limited liability company. It can include the name of the company, its purpose, the principal address of business, the Registered Agent's name and address, duration of the company, and its members.

Assets
Anything owned with monetary value. This includes both real and personal property.

Asset protection
A form of financial self-defense which places assets beyond the reach of creditors.

Authorized shares
The number of shares a corporation is authorized to sell.

Balance sheet
A financial statement that shows the true state of a particular business.

B-C

Bona Fida Occupational Qualifications (BFOQs)

Specific job requirements where religion, gender or national origin is an absolutely necessary qualification for the business to operate normally.

Boycott

To refrain from dealing with a particular business or industry.

Breach of contract

Failure without legal excuse to perform a promise contained in a valid contract, either written or oral.

Bulletproof statutes

State statutes governing LLC formation that, if followed, assure the LLC it will be taxed as a partnership for federal tax purposes.

Business name

Trade name or commercial name used to identify a specific business.

Bylaws

Rules adopted by the corporation itself for the regulation of a corporation's own actions; a subordinate law adopted by a corporation, association, or other body for its self-government or to regulate the rights and duties of its officers and members.

C corporation

A regular corporation that is not an S corporation.

Calendar year

The accounting year beginning on January 1 and ending on December 31.

Cash method

A financial record-keeping system relying on actual cash receipts or actual cash disbursements at the time of receipt or disbursement.

Certificate or Articles of Incorporation

The document that creates a corporation according to the laws of the state. This must be filed and approved by the state.

Certificate of Organization

The document that creates an LLC according to the laws of the state. This must be filed and approved by the state.

Charging order

A statutorily created means for a creditor of a judgment debtor who is a partner of others to reach the debtor's beneficial interest in the partnership, without risking dissolution of the partnership.

C-F

Consolidation
When two corporations combine, creating a third.

Corporation
A business formed and authorized by law to act as a single entity, although it may be owned by one or more persons. It is legally endowed with rights and responsibilities and has a life of its own independent of the owners and operators. The owners are not personally liable for debts or obligations of the corporation.

D.B.A. (Doing-Business-As) See "fictitious business name"

Deceptively similar
A name so similar to another name that the two become confused in the public eye.

Default rules
Statutory rules that take effect in the absence of contrary provisions in an Operating Agreement.

Dissolution
Formal statutory liquidation, termination and winding up of a business entity.

Distribution
Payment of cash or property to a member, shareholder or partner according to his or her percentage of ownership.

Dividend income
Dividends that must be declared as regular income for income tax purposes.

Double taxation
Occurs when corporations pay tax on corporate profits and shareholders pay income tax on dividend or distributive income.

Employer Identification Number (EIN)
A number issued by state and federal governments to identify a business for tax purposes. In a sole proprietorship, your Social Security Number serves as your EIN.

Employment-at-will
An employment relationship in which an employer has the right to fire an employee without notice.

Family limited partnership
A type of partnership that is comprised of lineal family members, usually with a parent as a general partner and children as limited partners.

Fictitious business name
A name other than the registered name under which a company may do business as long as it is not used for fraudulent purposes.

F-I

Fiscal year

Any 12-month period used by a business as its fiscal accounting period. Such accounting period may, for example, run from July 1 of one year through June 30 of the next year.

Flexible statutes

State formation statutes that allow an LLC options that exceed IRS guidelines for special tax status.

Foreign corporation

A corporation formed in one state or country but conducting some or all of its business in another state or country.

Foreign LLC

A limited liability company formed in one state or country but conducting some or all of its business in another state or country.

Free transfer of interests

The ability to transfer a membership interest to a non-member without consent of the other members.

General partner

The partner who accepts personal liability and is responsible for the daily management of a partnership.

Gift

For tax purposes, the IRS recognizes as a gift any voluntary transfer of property without consideration whose value does not exceed $10,000.

Incorporate

To form a corporation or to organize and be granted status as a corporation by following procedures prescribed by law.

Indemnification

Financial or other protection provided by an LLC or corporation to its members, managers, directors, officers and employees, which protects them against expenses and liabilities in lawsuits alleging they breached some duty in their service to, or on behalf of, the company.

Incorporate

To form a corporation or to organize and be granted status as a corporation by following procedures prescribed by law.

Incorporator

The person who signs the Articles of Incorporation upon petitioning the state for a corporate charter.

Insolvency

Being able to pay one's debts; bankruptcy

I-L

Issued shares
The number of shares actually sold by the corporation.

Intangible assets
Property that is not real or tangible property; nonphysical assets such as intellectual property, goodwill and franchises.

Intellectual property
A general term used to describe intangible property such as copyrights, patents, trademarks, and trade secrets.

Judgment creditor
A creditor who has obtained a court-ordered judgment against a debtor.

Judgment debtor
A debtor who has a court-ordered judgment against him.

Liability
The condition of being responsible for possible or actual loss, penalty, evil, expense, or burden; the state of being bound or obliged by law or justice to do, pay, or make good something.

Limited liability
The condition in LLCs and corporations that frees owners from being personally liable for debts and obligations of the company, with a few tax-related exceptions. In the case of company or corporate debt, general creditors cannot attach the owners' homes, cars and other personal property.

Limited liability company
A business entity created by legislation that offers its owners the limited personal liability of a corporation and the tax advantages of a partnership.

Limited liability partnership
A partnership entered into by members of the same professional occupation which allows all partners limited liability regarding any malpractice or mishandling of affairs by any other partner; all partners are still liable for their own actions.

Limited partner
A partner who contributes capital or property to the partnership and enjoys limited liability to the extent of his or her investment but who may not participate in the management of the partnership.

Limited partnership
A type of partnership where one general partner has complete liability and control of the business, and in which any number of limited partners can invest assets with limited liability and no control of the business.

M-P

Malpractice
Professional misconduct or unreasonable lack of skill; failure of one rendering professional services to exercise that degree of skill and learning by the average prudent, reputable member of that profession with the result of injury, loss, or damage to the recipient of those services.

Mediation
The action of a disinterested third party to reconcile the differences between disagreeing parties, the result of which is not legally binding.

Member
One who contributes capital, property or services to an LLC and in return, receives a membership interest in the company.

Membership interest
The right to vote, participate in management decisions and receive distributions from the company.

Merger
The absorption of one corporation by another.

Minority stockholder
One who owns or controls less than 50 percent of the stock in a corporation.

Minutes
Written records of formal proceedings of stockholders' and directors' meetings.

Non-par value stock
Shares of stock without specified value.

Not-for-profit corporation
A corporation organized for some charitable, civil, social or other purpose that does not entail the generation of profit or the distribution of its income to members, principals, shareholders, officers or others affiliated with it. Such corporations are accorded special treatment under the law for some purposes, including taxation.

Operating Agreement
A statement of the general principles of a limited liability company which combines information from the Articles of Organization with resolutions passed unanimously by members. It details economic and management arrangements as well as members' rights and responsibilities.

Oral agreement
Any unwritten contractual agreement between parties, not usually legally binding.

Parliamentary procedure
Rules such as "Roberts Rules of Order," which govern stockholders' meetings, directors' meetings, etc.

P-S

Par value stock

Shares of stock with a specified value.

Pass-through tax status

Profits that are not taxed on the company level but are distributed directly to members who report such profits as dividend income.

Proxy

Authorization by a stockholder allowing another to vote his shares of stock.

Publicly owned corporation

One whose stock is owned by more than 25 stockholders and is regulated by the Securities and Exchange Commission.

Quorum

A majority of the stockholders or directors necessary for vote-counting and decision-making at a meeting. While a quorum is usually a majority of either the total membership or the members present, a quorum may consist of a greater number than a simple majority if desired and stated in the bylaws.

Regular corporation

Also known as a C Corporation.

S Corporation (Subchapter S Corporation)

A small business corporation which elects to be taxed as a partnership or proprietorship for federal income tax purposes. Individual shareholders enjoy the benefits under state law of limited corporate liability, but avoid corporate federal taxes.

Securities

Stocks, bonds, notes, convertible debentures, warrants or other documents that represent a share in a company or a debt owed by a company or government entity.

Service business

A business that sells service or advice instead of a tangible product.

Shareholder

See Stockholder.

Silent partner

A dormant or limited partner; one whose name does not appear in the firm and who takes no active part in the business, but who has an interest in the concern and shares the profits.

Sole proprietorship

A business owned by an individual who is solely responsible for all aspects of the business; the business and its owners are thus considered to be the same entity.

S-W

Start-up venture
A new business having no track record.

State statutes
Laws created by a state legislature.

Statutory agent
A lawyer, corporation or individual who has assumed the responsibility of being the legal representative for the corporation for purposes of accepting legal service in a certain state.

S Corporation (Subchapter S Corporation)
A small business corporation which elects to be taxed as a partnership or proprietorship for federal income tax purposes. Individual shareholders enjoy the benefits under state law of limited corporate liability, but avoid corporate federal taxes.

Stock certificate
Written instrument evidencing a share in the ownership of a corporation.

Stockholder
A holder of one or more shares of the stock of a corporation. A stockholder may be called a "shareholder."

Subsidiary
A corporation owned by another corporation.

Substitute limited partner
One who purchases a limited partner's interest in a limited partnership.

Tangible assets
Real or personal property; assets with physical value, as distinguished from intangible property.

Tax basis
The value assigned to an asset for the purpose of determining income tax.

Uniform Limited Partnership Act
A set of regulations for limited partnerships adopted by most of the 50 states, the District of Columbia, and several U.S. territories with some modifications. There is also the Revised Limited Partnership Act.

Uniform Partnership Act
A set of regulations for partnerships adopted by most of the 50 states, the District of Columbia, and several U.S. territories with some modifications.

Wrongful discharge
Firing an employee without just cause.

Resources

••• Online Resources •••

◆ About.com
http://www.sbinformation.about.com

◆ AltaVista Small Business
*http://altavista.looksmart.com/eus1/eus65300/
eus65319/r?l&izf&*

◆ America's Business Funding Directory
http://www.business finance.com/search.asp

◆ AOL.COM Business & Careers
http://www.aol.com/webcenters/workplace/home.adp

◆ BizMove.com
http://www.bizmove.com

◆ Biztalk.com Small Business Community
http://www.biztalk.com

◆ Bplans.com!
http://www.bplans.com

◆ **BusinessTown.Com**
   http://www.businesstown.com

◆ **Council of Better Business Bureaus, Inc.**
   http://www.bbb.org

◆ **Education Index, Business Resources**
   http://www.educationindex.com/bus

◆ **Electric Library Business Edition**
   http://www.business.elibrary.com

◆ **EntrepreneurMag.com**
   http://www.entrepreneurmag.com

◆ **Federal Trade Commission-Franchise and Business Opportunities**
   http://www.ftc.gov/bcp/menu-fran.htm

◆ **HotBot Directory/Small Business**
   http://directory.hotbot.com/Business/Small_Business

◆ **Inc. Online**
   http://www.inc.com

◆ **Infoseek: Small Business**
   http://infoseek.go.com/Center/Business/Small_business

◆ **Internal Revenue Service**
   http://www.irs.ustreas.gov/prod/cover.html

◆ **International Finance & Commodities Institute**
   http://finance.wat.ch/IFCI

◆ **LNET-LLC-The Limited Liability Companies and Partnerships Conference**
   http://www.stcl.edu/lnet-llc/lnet-llc.html

◆ **Limited Liability Company Website**
   http://www.llcweb.com

- **Lycos Directory: Small Business**
  http://dir.lycos.com/Business/Small_Business

- **Netscape Women in Business**
  http://women.netscape.com/smallbusiness

- **National Association of Small Business Investment Companies**
  http://www.nasbic.org

- **National Foundation for Women Business Owners (NFWBO)**
  http://www.nfwbo.org

- **National Small Business Development Center (SBDC) Research Network**
  http://www.smallbiz.suny.edu

- **National Small Business Network Resource Directory**
  http://businessknowhow.net/Directory/bkhDindex.asp

- **National Small Business United**
  http://www.nsbu.org

- **North American Securities Administrators Association (NASAA)**
  http://www.nasaa.org

- **Occupational Safety and Health Administration (OSHA)**
  http://www.osha.gov

- **Service Core of Retired Executives**
  http://www.score.org

- **Small Business Advisor**
  http://www.isquare.com

- **Small Business Assistance, Environmental Protection Agency**
  http://es.epa.gov/new/business/business.html

◆ **Small Business Innovation Research (SBIR) Program**
  http://es.epa.gov/business/index.html

◆ **Small Business Primer**
  http://www.ces.ncsu.edu/depts/fcs/business/welcome.html

◆ **Small Business Resource**
  http://www.irl.co.uk/sbr

◆ **Small Business Taxes & Management**
  http://www.smbiz.com

◆ **Smalloffice.com**
  http://www.smalloffice.com

◆ **Tax and Accounting Sites Directory**
  http://www.taxsites.com

◆ **U.S. Business Advisor**
  http://www.business.gov

◆ **U.S. Chamber of Commerce**
  http://www.uschamber.org/smallbiz/index.html

◆ **U.S. Equal Employment Opportunity Commission's (EEOC)**
  http://www.eeoc.gov

◆ **U.S. Government Printing Office-Small Business**
  http://www.access.gpo.gov/su_docs/sale/sb-307.html

◆ **U.S. Small Business Administration**
  http://www.sbaonline.sba.gov

◆ **U.S. Treasury Department-Business Services**
  http://www.ustreas.gov/busserv.html

◆ **Webcrawler: Small Business**
  http://quicken.webcrawler.com/small_business

◆ **Yahoo! Business and Economy: Marketing**
http://dir.yahoo.com/Business_and_Economy/Marketing

◆ **Yahoo! Small Business**
http://smallbusiness.yahoo.com

••• Legal Search Engines •••

◆ **All Law**
http://www.alllaw.com

◆ **American Law Sources On Line**
http://www.lawsource.com/also/searchfm.htm

◆ **Catalaw**
http://www.catalaw.com

◆ **FindLaw**
http://www.findlaw.com

◆ **InternetOracle**
http://www.internetoracle.com/legal.htm

◆ **LawAid**
http://www.lawaid.com/search.html

◆ **LawCrawler**
http://www.lawcrawler.com

◆ **LawEngine, The**
http://www.fastsearch.com/law

◆ **LawRunner**
http://www.lawrunner.com

◆ **'Lectric Law Library™**
http://www.lectlaw.com

◆ **Legal Search Engines**
   http://www.dreamscape.com/frankvad/search.legal.html

◆ **LEXIS/NEXIS Communications Center**
   http://www.lexis-nexis.com/lncc/general/search.html

◆ **Meta-Index for U.S. Legal Research**
   http://gsulaw.gsu.edu/metaindex

◆ **Seamless Website, The**
   http://seamless.com

◆ **USALaw**
   http://www.usalaw.com/linksrch.cfm

◆ **WestLaw**
   http://westdoc.com (Registered users only. Fee paid service.)

••• State Bar Associations •••

ALABAMA
Alabama State Bar
415 Dexter Avenue
Montgomery, AL 36104

mailing address:
PO Box 671
Montgomery, AL 36101
(334) 269-1515

http://www.alabar.org

ALASKA
Alaska Bar Association
510 L Street No. 602
Anchorage, AK 99501

mailing address:
PO Box 100279
Anchorage, AK 99510

ARIZONA
State Bar of Arizona
111 West Monroe
Phoenix, AZ 85003-1742
(602) 252-4804

ARKANSAS
Arkansas Bar Association
400 West Markham
Little Rock, AR 72201
(501) 375-4605

CALIFORNIA
State Bar of California
555 Franklin Street
San Francisco, CA 94102
(415) 561-8200

http://www.calbar.org
Alameda County Bar
Association

http://www.acbanet.org

COLORADO
Colorado Bar Association
No. 950, 1900 Grant Street
Denver, CO 80203
(303) 860-1115
http://www.cobar.org

CONNECTICUT
Connecticut Bar Association
101 Corporate Place
Rocky Hill, CT 06067-1894
(203) 721-0025

DELAWARE
Delaware State Bar Association
1225 King Street, 10th floor
Wilmington, DE 19801
(302) 658-5279
(302) 658-5278 (lawyer referral
service)

DISTRICT OF COLUMBIA
District of Columbia Bar
1250 H Street, NW, 6th Floor
Washington, DC 20005
(202) 737-4700

Bar Association of the District of
Columbia
1819 H Street, NW, 12th floor
Washington, DC 20006-3690
(202) 223-6600

FLORIDA
The Florida Bar
The Florida Bar Center
650 Apalachee Parkway
Tallahassee, FL 32399-2300
(850) 561-5600

GEORGIA
State Bar of Georgia
800 The Hurt Building
50 Hurt Plaza
Atlanta, GA 30303
(404) 527-8700
http://www.gabar.org

HAWAII
Hawaii State Bar Association
1136 Union Mall
Penthouse 1
Honolulu, HI 96813
(808) 537-1868
http://www.hsba.org

IDAHO
Idaho State Bar
PO Box 895
Boise, ID 83701
(208) 334-4500

ILLINOIS
Illinois State Bar Association
424 South Second Street
Springfield, IL 62701
(217) 525-1760

INDIANA
Indiana State Bar Association
230 East Ohio Street
Indianapolis, IN 46204
(317) 639-5465
http://www.iquest.net/isba

IOWA
Iowa State Bar Association
521 East Locust
Des Moines, IA 50309
(515) 243-3179
http://www.iowabar.org

KANSAS
Kansas Bar Association
1200 Harrison Street
Topeka, KS 66601
(913) 234-5696
*http://www.ink.org/public/
cybar*

KENTUCKY
Kentucky Bar Association
514 West Main Street
Frankfort, KY 40601-1883
(502) 564-3795
http://www.kybar.org

LOUISIANA
Louisiana State Bar Association
601 St. Charles Avenue
New Orleans, LA 70130
(504) 566-1600

MAINE
Maine State Bar Association
124 State Street
PO Box 788
Augusta, ME 04330
(207) 622-7523

http://www.mainebar.org

MARYLAND
Maryland State Bar Association
520 West Fayette Street
Baltimore, MD 21201
(301) 685-7878

http://www.msba.org/msba

MASSACHUSETTS
Massachusetts Bar Association
20 West Street
Boston, MA 02111
(617) 542-3602
(617) 542-9103 (lawyer referral service)

MICHIGAN
State Bar of Michigan
306 Townsend Street
Lansing, MI 48933-2083
(517) 372-9030

http://www.michbar.org

MINNESOTA
Minnesota State Bar Association
514 Nicollet Mall
Minneapolis, MN 55402
(612) 333-1183

MISSISSIPPI
The Mississippi Bar
643 No. State Street
Jackson, Mississippi 39202
(601) 948-4471

MISSOURI
The Missouri Bar
P.O. Box 119, 326 Monroe
Jefferson City, Missouri 65102
(314) 635-4128

http://www.mobar.org

MONTANA
State Bar of Montana
46 North Main
PO Box 577
Helena, MT 59624
(406) 442-7660

NEBRASKA
Nebraska State Bar Association
635 South 14th Street, 2nd floor
Lincoln, NE 68508
(402) 475-7091

http://www.nebar.com

NEVADA
State Bar of Nevada
201 Las Vegas Blvd.
Las Vegas, NV 89101
(702) 382-2200

http://www.nvbar.org

NEW HAMPSHIRE
New Hampshire Bar Association
112 Pleasant Street
Concord, NH 03301
(603) 224-6942

NEW JERSEY
New Jersey State Bar Association
One Constitution Square
New Brunswick, NJ 08901-1500
(908) 249-5000

NEW MEXICO
State Bar of New Mexico
121 Tijeras Street N.E.
Albuquerque, NM 87102

mailing address:
PO Box 25883
Albuquerque, NM 87125
(505) 843-6132

NEW YORK
New York State Bar Association
One Elk Street
Albany, NY 12207
(518) 463-3200

http://www.nysba.org

NORTH CAROLINA
North Carolina State Bar
208 Fayetteville Street Mall
Raleigh, NC 27601

mailing address:
PO Box 25908
Raleigh, NC 27611
(919) 828-4620

North Carolina Bar Association
1312 Annapolis Drive
Raleigh, NC 27608

mailing address:
PO Box 12806
Raleigh, NC 27605
(919) 828-0561

http://www.barlinc.org

NORTH DAKOTA
State Bar Association of North
Dakota
515 1/2 East Broadway, suite 101
Bismarck, ND 58501

mailing address:
PO Box 2136
Bismarck, ND 58502
(701) 255-1404

OHIO
Ohio State Bar Association
1700 Lake Shore Drive
Columbus, OH 43204

mailing address:
PO Box 16562
Columbus, OH 43216-6562
(614) 487-2050

OKLAHOMA
Oklahoma Bar Association
1901 North Lincoln
Oklahoma City, OK 73105
(405) 524-2365

OREGON
Oregon State Bar
5200 S.W. Meadows Road
PO Box 1689
Lake Oswego, OR 97035-0889
(503) 620-0222

PENNSYLVANIA
Pennsylvania Bar Association
100 South Street
PO Box 186
Harrisburg, PA 17108
(717) 238-6715

Pennsylvania Bar Institute

http://www.pbi.org

PUERTO RICO
Puerto Rico Bar Association
PO Box 1900
San Juan, Puerto Rico 00903
(787) 721-3358

RHODE ISLAND
Rhode Island Bar Association
115 Cedar Street
Providence, RI 02903
(401) 421-5740

SOUTH CAROLINA
South Carolina Bar
950 Taylor Street
PO Box 608
Columbia, SC 29202
(803) 799-6653

http://www.scbar.org

SOUTH DAKOTA
State Bar of South Dakota
222 East Capitol
Pierre, SD 57501
(605) 224-7554

TENNESSEE
Tennessee Bar Assn
3622 West End Avenue
Nashville, TN 37205
(615) 383-7421

http://www.tba.org

TEXAS
State Bar of Texas
1414 Colorado
PO Box 12487
Austin, TX 78711
(512) 463-1463

UTAH
Utah State Bar
645 South 200 East, Suite 310
Salt Lake City, UT 84111
(801) 531-9077

VERMONT
Vermont Bar Association
PO Box 100
Montpelier, VT 05601
(802) 223-2020

VIRGINIA
Virginia State Bar
707 East Main Street, suite 1500
Richmond, VA 23219-0501
(804) 775-0500

Virginia Bar Association
701 East Franklin St., Suite 1120
Richmond, VA 23219
(804) 644-0041

VIRGIN ISLANDS
Virgin Islands Bar Association
P.O. Box 4108
Christiansted, Virgin Islands
00822
(340) 778-7497

WASHINGTON
Washington State Bar Association
500 Westin Street
2001 Sixth Avenue
Seattle, WA 98121-2599
(206) 727-8200

http://www.wsba.org

WEST VIRGINIA
West Virginia State Bar
2006 Kanawha Blvd. East
Charleston, WV 25311
(304) 558-2456

http://www.wvbar.org

West Virginia Bar Association
904 Security Building
100 Capitol Street
Charleston, WV 25301
(304) 342-1474

WISCONSIN
State Bar of Wisconsin
402 West Wilson Street
Madison, WI 53703
(608) 257-3838

http://www.wisbar.org/
home.htm

WYOMING
Wyoming State Bar
500 Randall Avenue
Cheyenne, WY 82001
PO Box 109
Cheyenne, WY 82003
(307) 632-9061

How to save on attorney fees

How to save on attorney fees

Millions of Americans know they need legal protection, whether it's to get agreements in writing, protect themselves from lawsuits, or document business transactions. But too often these basic but important legal matters are neglected because of something else millions of Americans know: legal services are expensive.

They don't have to be. In response to the demand for affordable legal protection and services, there are now specialized clinics that process simple documents. Paralegals help people prepare legal claims on a freelance basis. People find they can handle their own legal affairs with do-it-yourself legal guides and kits. Indeed, this book is a part of this growing trend.

When are these alternatives to a lawyer appropriate? If you hire an attorney, how can you make sure you're getting good advice for a reasonable fee? Most importantly, do you know how to lower your legal expenses?

When there is no alternative

Make no mistake: serious legal matters require a lawyer. The tips in this book can help you reduce your legal fees, but there is no alternative to good professional legal services in certain circumstances:

- when you are charged with a felony, you are a repeat offender, or jail is possible

- when a substantial amount of money or property is at stake in a lawsuit

- when you are a party in an adversarial divorce or custody case

- when you are an alien facing deportation

- when you are the plaintiff in a personal injury suit that involves large sums of money

- when you're involved in very important transactions

Are you sure you want to take it to court?

Consider the following questions before you pursue legal action:

What are your financial resources?

Money buys experienced attorneys, and experience wins over first-year lawyers and public defenders. Even with a strong case, you may save money by not going to court. Yes, people win millions in court. But for every big winner there are ten plaintiffs who either lose or win so little that litigation wasn't worth their effort.

Do you have the time and energy for a trial?

Courts are overbooked, and by the time your case is heard your initial zeal may have grown cold. If you can, make a reasonable settlement out of court. On personal matters, like a divorce or custody case, consider the emotional toll on all parties. Any legal case will affect you in some way. You will need time away from work. A newsworthy case may bring press coverage. Your loved ones, too, may face publicity. There is usually good reason to settle most cases quickly, quietly, and economically.

How can you settle disputes without litigation?

Consider *mediation*. In mediation, each party pays half the mediator's fee and, together, they attempt to work out a compromise informally. *Binding arbitration* is another alternative. For a small fee, a trained specialist serves as judge, hears both sides, and hands down a ruling that both parties have agreed to accept.

So you need an attorney

Having done your best to avoid litigation, if you still find yourself headed for court, you will need an attorney. To get the right attorney at a reasonable cost, be guided by these four questions:

What type of case is it?

You don't seek a foot doctor for a toothache. Find an attorney experienced in your type of legal problem. If you can get recommendations from clients who have recently won similar cases, do so.

Where will the trial be held?

You want a lawyer familiar with that court system and one who knows the court personnel and the local protocol—which can vary from one locality to another.

Should you hire a large or small firm?

Hiring a senior partner at a large and prestigious law firm sounds reassuring, but chances are the actual work will be handled by associates—at high rates. Small firms may give your case more attention but, with fewer resources, take longer to get the work done.

What can you afford?

Hire an attorney you can afford, of course, but know what a fee quote includes. High fees may reflect a firm's luxurious offices, high-paid staff and unmonitored expenses, while low estimates may mean "unexpected" costs later. Ask for a written estimate of all costs and anticipated expenses.

How to find a good lawyer

Whether you need an attorney quickly or you're simply open to future possibilities, here are seven nontraditional methods for finding your lawyer:

1) **Word of mouth**: Successful lawyers develop reputations. Your friends, business associates and other professionals are potential referral sources. But beware of hiring a friend. Keep the client-attorney relationship strictly business.

2) **Directories**: The Yellow Pages and the Martin-Hubbell Lawyer Directory (in your local library) can help you locate a lawyer with the right education, background and expertise for your case.

3) **Databases**: A paralegal should be able to run a quick computer search of local attorneys for you using the Westlaw or Lexis database.

4) **State bar associations**: Bar associations are listed in phone books. Along with lawyer referrals, your bar association can direct you to low-cost legal clinics or specialists in your area.

5) **Law schools**: Did you know that a legal clinic run by a law school gives law students hands-on experience? This may fit your legal needs. A third-year law student loaded with enthusiasm and a little experience might fill the bill quite inexpensively—or even for free.

6) **Advertisements:** Ads are a lawyer's business card. If a "TV attorney" seems to have a good track record with your kind of case, why not call? Just don't be swayed by the glamour of a high-profile attorney.

7) **Your own ad:** A small ad describing the qualifications and legal expertise you're seeking, placed in a local bar association journal, may get you just the lead you need.

How to hire and work with your attorney

No matter how you hear about an attorney, you must interview him or her in person. Call the office during business hours and ask to speak to the attorney directly. Then explain your case briefly and mention how you obtained the attorney's name. If the attorney sounds interested and knowledgeable, arrange for a visit.

The ten-point visit

1) Note the address. This is a good indication of the rates to expect.

2) Note the condition of the offices. File-laden desks and poorly maintained work space may indicate a poorly run firm.

3) Look for up-to-date computer equipment and an adequate complement of support personnel.

4) Note the appearance of the attorney. How will he or she impress a judge or jury?

5) Is the attorney attentive? Does the attorney take notes, ask questions, follow up on points you've mentioned?

6)   Ask what schools he or she has graduated from, and feel free to check credentials with the state bar association.

7)   Does the attorney have a good track record with your type of case?

8)   Does he or she explain legal terms to you in plain English?

9)   Are the firm's costs reasonable?

10) Will the attorney provide references?

Hiring the attorney

Having chosen your attorney, make sure all the terms are agreeable. Send letters to any other attorneys you have interviewed, thanking them for their time and interest in your case and explaining that you have retained another attorney's services.

Request a letter from your new attorney outlining your retainer agreement. The letter should list all fees you will be responsible for as well as the billing arrangement. Did you arrange to pay in installments? This should be noted in your retainer agreement.

Controlling legal costs

Legal fees and expenses can get out of control easily, but the client who is willing to put in the effort can keep legal costs manageable. Work out a budget with your attorney. Create a timeline for your case. Estimate the costs involved in each step.

Legal fees can be straightforward. Some lawyers charge a fixed rate for a specific project. Others charge contingency fees (they collect a percentage of your recovery, usually 35-50 percent if you win and nothing if you lose). But most attorneys prefer to bill by the hour. Expenses can run the gamut, with one hourly charge for taking depositions and another for making copies.

Have your attorney give you a list of charges for services rendered and an itemized monthly bill. The bill should explain the service performed, who performed the work, when the service was provided, how long it took, and how the service benefits your case.

Ample opportunity abounds in legal billing for dishonesty and greed. There is also plenty of opportunity for knowledgeable clients to cut their bills significantly if they know what to look for. Asking the right questions and setting limits on fees is smart and can save you a bundle. Don't be afraid to question legal bills. It's your case and your money!

When the bill arrives

- **Retainer fees**: You should already have a written retainer agreement. Ideally, the retainer fee applies toward case costs, and your agreement puts that in writing. Protect yourself by escrowing the retainer fee until the case has been handled to your satisfaction.

- **Office visit charges**: Track your case and all documents, correspondence, and bills. Diary all dates, deadlines and questions you want to ask your attorney during your next office visit. This keeps expensive office visits focused and productive, with more accomplished in less time. If your attorney charges less for phone consultations than office visits, reserve visits for those tasks that must be done in person.

- **Phone bills**: This is where itemized bills are essential. Who made the call, who was spoken to, what was discussed, when was the call made, and how long did it last? Question any charges that seem unnecessary or excessive (over 60 minutes).

- **Administrative costs**: Your case may involve hundreds, if not thousands, of documents: motions, affidavits, depositions, interrogatories, bills, memoranda, and letters. Are they all necessary? Understand your attorney's case strategy before paying for an endless stream of costly documents.

- **Associate and paralegal fees**: Note in your retainer agreement which staff people will have access to your file. Then you'll have an informed and efficient staff working on your case, and you'll recognize their names on your bill. Of course, your attorney should handle the important part of your case, but less costly paralegals or associates may handle routine matters more economically. Note: Some firms expect their associates to meet a quota of billable hours, although the time spent is not always warranted. Review your bill. Does the time spent make sense for the document in question? Are several staff involved in matters that should be handled by one person? Don't be afraid to ask questions. And withhold payment until you have satisfactory answers.

- **Court stenographer fees**: Depositions and court hearings require costly transcripts and stenographers. This means added expenses. Keep an eye on these costs.

- **Copying charges**: Your retainer fee should limit the number of copies made of your complete file. This is in your legal interest, because multiple files mean multiple chances others may access your confidential information. It is also in your financial interest, because copying costs can be astronomical.

- **Fax costs**: As with the phone and copier, the fax can easily run up costs. Set a limit.

- **Postage charges**: Be aware of how much it costs to send a legal document overnight, or a registered letter. Offer to pick up or deliver expensive items when it makes sense.

- **Filing fees**: Make it clear to your attorney that you want to minimize the number of court filings in your case. Watch your bill and question any filing that seems unnecessary.

- **Document production fee**: Turning over documents to your opponent is mandatory and expensive. If you're faced with reproducing boxes of documents, consider having the job done by a commercial firm rather than your attorney's office.

- **Research and investigations**: Pay only for photographs that can be used in court. Can you hire a photographer at a lower rate than what your attorney charges? Reserve that right in your retainer agreement. Database research can also be extensive and expensive; if your attorney uses Westlaw or Nexis, set limits on the research you will pay for.

- **Expert witnesses**: Question your attorney if you are expected to pay for more than a reasonable number of expert witnesses. Limit the number to what is essential to your case.

- **Technology costs**: Avoid videos, tape recordings, and graphics if you can use old-fashioned diagrams to illustrate your case.

- **Travel expenses**: Travel expenses for those connected to your case can be quite costly unless you set a maximum budget. Check all travel-related items on your bill, and make sure they are appropriate. Always question why the travel is necessary before you agree to pay for it.

- **Appeals costs**: Losing a case often means an appeal, but weigh the costs involved before you make that decision. If money is at stake, do a cost-benefit analysis to see if an appeal is financially justified.

- **Monetary damages**: Your attorney should be able to help you estimate the total damages you will have to pay if you lose a civil case. Always consider settling out of court rather than proceeding to trial when the trial costs will be high.

- **Surprise costs**: Surprise costs are so routine they're predictable. The judge may impose unexpected court orders on one or both sides, or the opposition will file an unexpected motion that increases your legal costs. Budget a few thousand dollars over what you estimate your case will cost. It usually is needed.

- **Padded expenses**: Assume your costs and expenses are legitimate. But some firms do inflate expenses—office supplies, database searches, copying, postage, phone bills—to bolster their bottom line. Request copies of bills your law firm receives from support services. If you are not the only client represented on a bill, determine those charges related to your case.

Keeping it legal without a lawyer

The best way to save legal costs is to avoid legal problems. There are hundreds of ways to decrease your chances of lawsuits and other nasty legal encounters. Most simply involve a little common sense. You can also use your own initiative to find and use the variety of self-help legal aid available to consumers.

11 situations in which you may not need a lawyer

1) **No-fault divorce**: Married couples with no children, minimal property, and no demands for alimony can take advantage of divorce mediation services. A lawyer should review your divorce agreement before you sign it, but you will have saved a fortune in attorney fees. A marital or family counselor may save a seemingly doomed marriage, or help both parties move beyond anger to a calm settlement. Either way, counseling can save you money.

2) **Wills**: Do-it-yourself wills and living trusts are ideal for people with estates of less than $600,000. Even if an attorney reviews your final documents, a will kit allows you to read the documents, ponder your bequests, fill out sample forms, and discuss your wishes with your family at your leisure, without a lawyer's meter running.

3) **Incorporating**: Incorporating a small business can be done by any business owner. Your state government office provides the forms and instructions necessary. A visit to your state office will probably be

necessary to perform a business name check. A fee of $100-$200 is usually charged for processing your Articles of Incorporation. The rest is paperwork: filling out forms correctly; holding regular, official meetings; and maintaining accurate records.

4) **Routine business transactions**: Copyrights, for example, can be applied for by asking the U.S. Copyright Office for the appropriate forms and brochures. The same is true of the U.S. Patent and Trademark Office. If your business does a great deal of document preparation and research, hire a certified paralegal rather than paying an attorney's rates. Consider mediation or binding arbitration rather than going to court for a business dispute. Hire a human resources/benefits administrator to head off disputes concerning discrimination or other employee charges.

5) **Repairing bad credit**: When money matters get out of hand, attorneys and bankruptcy should not be your first solution. Contact a credit counseling organization that will help you work out manageable payment plans so that everyone wins. It can also help you learn to manage your money better. A good company to start with is the Consumer Credit Counseling Service, 1-800-388-2227.

6) **Small Claims Court**: For legal grievances amounting to a few thousand dollars in damages, represent yourself in Small Claims Court. There is a small filing fee, forms to fill out, and several court visits necessary. If you can collect evidence, state your case in a clear and logical presentation, and come across as neat, respectful and sincere, you can succeed in Small Claims Court.

7) **Traffic Court**: Like Small Claims Court, Traffic Court may show more compassion to a defendant appearing without an attorney. If you are ticketed for a minor offense and want to take it to court, you will be asked to plead guilty or not guilty. If you plead guilty, you can ask for leniency in sentencing by presenting mitigating circumstances. Bring any witnesses who can support your story, and remember that presentation (some would call it acting ability) is as important as fact.

8) **Residential zoning petition**: If a homeowner wants to open a home business, build an addition, or make other changes that may affect his or her neighborhood, town approval is required. But you don't need a lawyer to fill out a zoning variance application, turn it in, and present your story at a public hearing. Getting local support before the hearing is the best way to assure a positive vote; contact as many neighbors as possible to reassure them that your plans won't adversely affect them or the neighborhood.

9) **Government benefit applications**: Applying for veterans' or unemployment benefits may be daunting, but the process doesn't require legal help. Apply for either immediately upon becoming eligible. Note: If your former employer contests your application for unemployment benefits and you have to defend yourself at a hearing, you may want to consider hiring an attorney.

10) **Receiving government files**: The Freedom of Information Act gives every American the right to receive copies of government information about him or her. Write a letter to the appropriate state or federal agency, noting the precise information you want. List each document in a separate paragraph. Mention the Freedom of Information Act, and state that you will pay any expenses. Close with your signature and the address the documents should be sent to. An approved request may take six months to arrive. If it is refused on the grounds that the information is classified or violates another's privacy, send a letter of appeal explaining why the released information would not endanger anyone. Enlist the support of your local state or federal representative, if possible, to smooth the approval process.

11) **Citizenship**: Arriving in the United States to work and become a citizen is a process tangled in bureaucratic red tape, but it requires more perseverance than legal assistance. Immigrants can learn how to obtain a "Green Card," under what circumstances they can work, and what the requirements of citizenship are by contacting the Immigration Services or reading a good self-help book.

Save more; it's E-Z

When it comes to saving attorneys' fees, E-Z Legal Forms is the consumer's best friend. America's largest publisher of self-help legal products offers legally valid forms for virtually every situation. E-Z Legal Kits and E-Z Legal Guides include all necessary forms with a simple-to-follow manual of instructions or a layman's book. E-Z Legal Books are a legal library of forms and documents for everyday business and personal needs. E-Z Legal Software provides those same forms on disk and CD for customized documents at the touch of the keyboard.

You can add to your legal savvy and your ability to protect yourself, your loved ones, your business and your property with a range of self-help legal titles available through E-Z Legal Forms. See the product descriptions and information at the back of this guide.

Whatever you need to know, we've made it E-Z!

Informative text and forms you can fill out on-screen.* From personal to business, legal to leisure—we've made it E-Z!

PERSONAL & FAMILY

For all your family's needs, we have titles that will help keep you organized and guide you through most every aspect of your personal life.

BUSINESS

Whether you're starting from scratch with a home business or you just want to keep your corporate records in shape, we've got the programs for you.

By the book...

	Item#	Qty.	Price Ea.‡
★ **Made E◆Z Software**			
Accounting Made E-Z	SW1207		$29.95
Asset Protection Made E-Z	SW1157		$29.95
Bankruptcy Made E-Z	SW1154		$29.95
Business Startups Made E-Z	SW1192		$29.95
Buying/Selling Your Home Made E-Z	SW1213		$29.95
Car Buying Made E-Z	SW1146		$29.95
Corporate Record Keeping Made E-Z	SW1159		$29.95
Credit Repair Made E-Z	SW1153		$29.95
Divorce Law Made E-Z	SW1182		$29.95
Everyday Law Made E-Z	SW1185		$29.95
Everyday Legal Forms & Agreements	SW1186		$29.95
Incorporation Made E-Z	SW1176		$29.95
Last Wills Made E-Z	SW1177		$29.95
Living Trusts Made E-Z	SW1178		$29.95
Offshore Investing Made E-Z	SW1218		$29.95
Owning a Franchise Made E-Z	SW1202		$29.95
Your Profitable Home Business	SW1204		$29.95
★ **Made E◆Z Guides**			
Bankruptcy Made E-Z	G200		$17.95
Incorporation Made E-Z	G201		$17.95
Divorce Law Made E-Z	G202		$17.95
Credit Repair Made E-Z	G203		$17.95
Living Trusts Made E-Z	G205		$17.95
Living Wills Made E-Z	G206		$17.95
Last Wills Made E-Z	G207		$17.95
Small Claims Court Made E-Z	G209		$17.95
Traffic Court Made E-Z	G210		$17.95
Buying/Selling Your Home Made E-Z	G211		$17.95
Employment Law Made E-Z	G212		$17.95
Immigration Made E-Z	G213		$17.95
Collecting Child Support Made E-Z	G215		$17.95
Limited Liability Companies Made E-Z	G216		$17.95
Partnerships Made E-Z	G218		$17.95
Solving IRS Problems Made E-Z	G219		$17.95
Asset Protection Made E-Z	G220		$17.95
Buying/Selling A Business Made E-Z	G221		$17.95
Raising Venture Capital Made E-Z	G222		$17.95
Profitable Mail Order Made E-Z	G223		$17.95
E-Commerce Made E-Z	G224		$17.95
SBA Loans Made E-Z	G225		$17.95
Troubleshooting Your Business Made E-Z	G226		$17.95
Advertising & Promoting Your Business	G227		$17.95
Rapid Reading Made E-Z	G228		$17.95
Everyday Math Made E-Z	G229		$17.95
Shoestring Investing Made E-Z	G230		$17.95
Stock Market Investing Made E-Z	G231		$17.95
Fundraising Made E-Z	G232		$17.95
Stop Smoking Made E-Z	G233		$17.95
College Funding Made E-Z	G234		$17.95
Marketing Your Small Business	G235		$17.95
Owning A No-Cash-Down Business	G236		$17.95
Offshore Investing Made E-Z	G237		$17.95
M-L-M Made E-Z	G238		$17.95
Free Legal Help Made E-Z	G239		$17.95
Free Stuff For Everyone Made E-Z	G240		$17.95
Your Profitable Home Business Made E-Z	G241		$17.95
Business Plans Made E-Z	G242		$17.95
Mutual Fund Investing Made E-Z	G243		$17.95
★ **Made E◆Z Books**			
Managing Employees Made E-Z	BK308		$29.95
Corporate Record Keeping Made E-Z	BK310		$29.95
Vital Record Keeping Made E-Z	BK312		$29.95
Business Forms Made E-Z	BK313		$29.95
Collecting Unpaid Bills Made E-Z	BK309		$29.95
Everyday Law Made E-Z	BK311		$29.95
Everyday Legal Forms & Agreements	BK307		$29.95
★ SHIPPING & HANDLING *			$
Florida Residents add 6% sales tax			$
TOTAL OF ORDER			$

ss 2000.r3

Index

O-W•••••